CUBA
FOR THE MISINFORMED

FACTS FROM THE
FORBIDDEN* ISLAND

MICK WINTER

*but only if you're an American

Cuba for the Misinformed
Facts from the Forbidden* Island
*but only if you're an American

Copyright © 2013 by Mick Winter

Published by
Westsong Publishing
Napa CA 94558
www.westsongpublishing.com

First print edition published 2013
ISBN 978-0-9659000-9-6

Library of Congress Control Number: 2013900740

"Cuba has the same effect on American administrations that the full moon has on werewolves."

–Wayne Smith, former head of
US Interests Section in Havana.

"Homeland is humanity"

On a Cuban billboard
–From the writings of José Martí

Dedication

To Martha Vega, mi profesora,

...and to all the people of Cuba, with gratitude,
for showing us what is possible.

Acknowledgments

My thanks to Marshall Soules, Suzanne Shiff, Bill Hackwell, Barry Evans and Hajo Hadeler for their contributions to this book, to Nancy Shapiro for her wonderful book cover, to my wife Kathryn Winter for her support and desperately needed advice and suggestions, and to all the photographers who generously contributed their work, particularly Adam Jones and his beautiful cover photo. I couldn't have done this without any of you. Any flaws in this book are totally mine . . . but they didn't result from lack of passion.

Where no photo credit is provided, photographs are by the author.

Cover design: Nancy Shapiro
Front photo: Adam Jones / adamjones.freeservers.com
Back photo: Alberto Korda

TABLE OF CONTENTS

Cuba for the Misinformed

Introduction

Americans have never been given a clear picture of what Cuba is *actually* like. The picture provided to Americans by the US government and by the mass media in the United States is very different from the real Cuba.

As Ricardo Alarcón, President of the Cuban National Assembly, has said, "There are two Cubas: ours and the one you picture to yourselves." [1] This book is intended to help eliminate, or at least decrease, the gap between those two pictures.

After you have seen the facts, you will recognize that something very interesting has been happening for more than fifty years just ninety miles offshore from the United States. Cuba is not just an interesting place to visit but is an exemplar for developed as well as developing countries all over the world. You may not agree with everything—or, depending on your political and social preferences, even *anything*—that has happened in Cuba since its revolution, but you will likely admit that this small island country of eleven million people has had a global effect that reaches far beyond its size.

This book is a compilation of facts, data, statistics and other information. It is not meant to be an in-depth scholarly work, a history, or a comprehensive guide for visitors to Cuba. It is simply a presentation of information that is little-known (particularly to most Americans) about Cuba and, in particular, its relationship to the United States. It should be of special interest not just to Americans but throughout the world to students, educators and others who wish to know more about Cuba.

Almost all of the information here is publicly available. Whenever possible, sources are documented in this book. The information derives from books, the Internet, newspaper articles, US government documents and agencies—including the Central Intelligence Agency—and reports from a variety of international organizations, including the United Nations and the World Bank.

Some of the information in the book comes from my direct experience. I was fortunate enough some years ago to spend a month studying Spanish at the University of Havana. The experience included cultural, economic, art, health and agricultural presentations, and was sponsored by Global Exchange[2], a

---

[1] Ricardo Alarcón, President of the Cuban National Assembly (2007) http://bit.ly/WbJmrU

[2] www.globalexchange.org

Cuba for the Misinformed

California non-profit dedicated to expanding awareness of countries and peoples around the world.

I have organized the book into general subject areas. These subject areas are for ease of navigation, and are not intended to be comprehensive. I have listed other resources at the back of the book. I recommend these books and websites for learning more about Cuba, its history, and what to see and do if you visit.

Where appropriate, I have also added footnotes with links to websites or publications where original and/or expanded information can be found. You will also find a comprehensive index at the end of the book.

Before Castro, there was Cuba. After Castro, there will be Cuba

Only in the fevered minds of aging—and vanishing—Cuban exiles in Florida, and in the fantasies of nostalgic Cold Warriors, does the hope exist that somehow Cuba after Castro (any Castro) will be transformed into a capitalist paradise, as the long-enslaved Cubans throw off their chains, rise up against Fidel and his brother Raúl, and once again make Cuba safe for American-style democracy. That is, safe for corporations, the financial industry, McDonald's, mining and oil companies, hotel chains, fast-food outlets, and advertising. An added advantage for the US government would be the elimination of the extensive social safety net currently enjoyed by Cuba's people, which, in the US government's eyes, serves as an undesirable example to the American people.

Successive American governments have preferred to believe that one man—the *Evil Bearded One*—has single-handedly enslaved the suffering Cuban people, and that once he and his brother have faded into history, all will be well again.

Cuba is a social experiment, a Caribbean Petri dish, a fifty-year pilot project for the planet, one in which the scientists inhabit the same dish that contains the organisms they study. Not everyone is happy with the experiment. Certainly not everyone in the dish is pleased to be there. The country to Cuba's north, generally considered to be the richest and most powerful empire in the history of the planet, appears terrified by its tiny neighbor.

The United States has devoted much energy trying to kill or devalue Fidel Castro, the lead scientist for the Cuban experiment. Why this is so is puzzling. Why would a country of more than 300 million people, armed to the teeth with multiple units of every weapon imaginable, fear a poor, tropical country of 11 million people?

There is precedent for this imagined fear. During the Reagan administration's attempts to counter the Sandinista revolution in Nicaragua, President Reagan stated: "The Sandinistas are just two days' drive from Harlingen, Texas." [3] [4] It mattered little that only one in 100,000 (at best) Americans knew where Harlingen was or that Nicaragua was 1,700 miles away—with Honduras, Guatemala and Mexico in-between. They knew Harlingen was on American soil and hence should never be despoiled.

The US government knows that Cuba is no military threat. But it is a threat by example. Cuba's refusal to be a pawn has infuriated the US government for more than five decades.

It began with Cuba's nationalization of foreign-owned corporations, its insistence on having a government that was no longer subservient to Washington, D.C., and its eviction of the US Mafia from Havana. Cuba then began to offer social benefits to its citizens, including sixteen or more years of free education, universal health care, and subsidized food and housing.

These ideas have continued to spread, inspiring changes in Venezuela, Bolivia, Ecuador and other countries. Cuba even helped the people of South Africa to throw out the US-supported apartheid government through its participation in defeating the South African army in Angola. The result has been continuing efforts by the US government to overthrow Cuba's socialist government and bring it back into the capitalist fold dominated by the United States.

Those efforts have failed.

The American government's antagonism towards Cuba is more than unfortunate; it is tragic. The Cuban society is a remarkable experiment, and it is even more remarkable that it has remained steadfast against its powerful antagonist to the north.

Cuba's problems are many. The opposition of the United States has been formidable, with both physical attacks and a blockade lasting for fifty years. Cuba's colonial history and limited resources have created a situation difficult to overcome. Cuba's revolutionary government has made many unfortunate decisions based on a rigid adherence to dogma, a mistake committed by many countries. To top it off, almost every year devastating hurricanes sweep through the island. One result is the heavy destruction of an already limited and deteriorating housing stock.

Despite its achievements, Cuba remains a developing nation in terms of resources and personal income. Everyone is housed, but most housing is below standard, often far below. Food is limited, and basic living essentials are often scarce. In terms of consumer lifestyle, Cuba suffers by comparison

---

[3] Houston Chronicle http://bit.ly/VUE1Vo

[4] The Day (New London, CT) http://bit.ly/Ry4fzm

Cuba for the Misinformed

to the United States; not surprisingly, since any underdeveloped country suffers when compared to the US economy and its consumer goods.

It is not, however, the United States to which Cuba should be compared— although those comparisons are frequently very favorable to Cuba. Even restricting the comparison just to the Americas, Cuba shines in relationship to the rest of the Caribbean, Central and South America—not to mention Africa and much of Asia.

Unfortunately, the work of the Cuban people has not been supported by the United States. But it has been supported by most of Cuba's own people. Cuba may be limited in physical resources, but it is exuberantly rich in the quality of its human capital, thanks to its educational policies and the initiative and dedication of the Cuban people. Had the United States attempted to assist the Cuban experiment rather than continually try to derail it, the accomplishments of Cuba's people could also have served the people of the United States. Cuba's commitment to sustainability, to international service, to the elimination of racism, and to the health, well-being and education of peoples throughout the world should have been supported and emulated, not thwarted.

We in the United States and elsewhere can learn much from what the Cuban people have accomplished. But we can learn only if we are aware of the facts.

Mick Winter
Napa, California

What's the Problem with Cuba?

When Lars Schoultz, professor of Political Science at the University of North Carolina at Chapel Hill and a past president of the Latin American Studies Association, was interviewed about his book *That Infernal Little Cuban Republic: The United States and the Cuban Revolution* (University of North Carolina Press, 2009), he said:

> The book's title [*That Infernal Little Cuban Republic*], taken from one of Theodore Roosevelt's letters in 1907, captures perfectly the exasperation of US officials since our first encounters in the early 1820s, when Havana-based pirates were plundering US shipping.
>
> But while Cuba has always been a pain in the neck, Fidel Castro's revolutionary generation—the focus of my book—has been especially annoying. It has sent us wave after wave of refugees. It has also supported governments and political movements we oppose in Latin America and Africa and even the Middle East, as if we didn't have enough problems there already. And most galling, it has refused to accept the position of inferiority to which we have traditionally assigned the peoples of the Caribbean. The Cuban revolution is a challenge to US hegemony, and as one White House official commented in the late 1960s, "that especially bugs us." [5]

---

[5] http://bit.ly/Us9H4s

Cuba in Caribbean
CREDIT: STANFORD UNIVERSITY

Where is Cuba?

Cuba is located in the northern Caribbean at the confluence of the Caribbean Sea, the Gulf of Mexico and the Atlantic Ocean. The island lies about 94 miles (151 kilometers) south of Key West, Florida The city of Havana is 228 miles (367 kilometers) southwest of the city of Miami. Cuba is east of Mexico, specifically the Yucatan Peninsula, and north of Jamaica.

Cuba's official name is *the Republic of Cuba*. It consists of the main island of Cuba, which is two-thirds the size of Florida, the Isle of Youth (*Isla de la Juventud*), and 4,195 small islands and keys (*cayos*).

Cuba is by far the largest island in the Caribbean, and its main island is the sixteenth largest island in the world, more than three times the size of Vancouver Island in Canada's province of British Columbia, and ten times the size of Hawaii's Big Island.

The country has a total land area of 42,426 square miles (109,884 square kilometers) with 2,320 miles (3,735 kilometers) of coastline, and its total land area is slightly smaller than the state of Pennsylvania. The terrain is mostly flat to rolling plains, with rugged hills and mountains in the southeast. Altitudes range from sea level to 6,578 feet (2,005 meters.) The longest river is the Cauto, 230 miles (370 kilometers) long.

The United States leases a naval base at Guantánamo Bay in the southeast corner of the island. The lease to this land was given by the Cuban government in 1903, a government installed by the United States. The lease continues until both Cuba and the United States *mutually* consent to terminate it. Cuba's consent is a given; it just needs the United States to agree to pull out.

Cuba has a tropical climate that is moderated by the surrounding waters of the Atlantic and the Caribbean. The warm waters, however, also cause Cuba to be hit by frequent hurricanes.

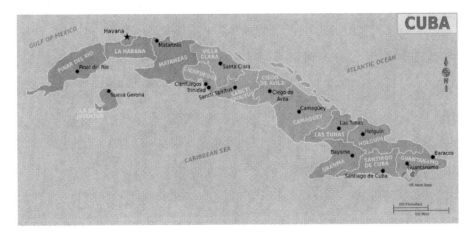

Cuban provinces
CREDIT: CACAHUATE/WIKIMEDIA COMMONS

History

Foreign powers have tried to control Cuba for its entire modern history. Columbus was the first European, but hardly the last. His "discovery" of Cuba turned that island into a Spanish colony which lasted, with only brief interruptions, until the so-called Spanish-American War of 1898. In this war, just as Cuban forces were decisively defeating Spanish troops, the Americans stepped in and took not just credit for the victory but control of the country. The US government "oversaw" Cuba for the next 61 years until the successful Revolution led by Fidel Castro and others. The Americans have been unhappy about their loss ever since.

Christopher Columbus

Christopher Columbus admired the native Cubans—then killed them

In 1492, when Christopher Columbus—known in Latin America by his Spanish name Cristobal Colón—encountered the inhabitants of the Caribbean—now known as the *Taino* (and also referred to as the *Arawak*)—he described them as "very well made, with handsome bodies, and very good countenances."

So impressed was Columbus with these people, which included those on Cuba, that his men immediately started enslaving them. Hundreds of thousands died within the next few decades as a result of European diseases and Spanish cruelty in the mines and plantations.

Spanish priest Bartolomé De Las Casas, who in 1542 wrote "A Short Account of the Destruction of the Indies," described the fate of one Taino village of about 2,500 people:

Cuba for the Misinformed

Christopher Columbus (Cristóbal Colón)
by Sebastiano del Piombo
CREDIT: WIKIMEDIA COMMONS

The Taino welcomed the Spaniards, and gave them food and drink. Once the feast was over, the Spanish "set upon the Indians," De Las Casas wrote, "slashing, disemboweling and slaughtering them until their blood ran like a river."

For those natives who were sent to the mines rather than immediately killed, De Las Casas also wrote that the Spanish "required of them tasks utterly beyond their strength, bending them to the earth with crushing burdens, harnessing them to loads which they could not drag, and with fiendish sport and mockery, hacking off their hands and feet, and mutilating their bodies in ways which will not bear description." [6]

---

[6] www.historyofcuba.com

Arawak (also known as Taino) woman
by John Gabriel Stedman.
CREDIT: WIKIMEDIA COMMONS

Hatuey

Chief Hatuey turned down Heaven

One victim of the Spanish was Chief Hatuey, who had led a revolt against the Spanish on the island of Hispaniola and then fled to Cuba to warn the native Taino there. He was captured by the Spanish. On February 2, 1512, just before he was to be burned at the stake, he was asked by a Spanish Franciscan friar if he wanted to accept Jesus, and go to heaven.

Hatuey asked the friar where Christians like him went when they died. The friar replied that they went to heaven. Hatuey responded that he would rather go where the Christians were not, declined the offer, and went to the stake unChristianized.

Chief Hatuey monument, Baracoa, Cuba.
CREDIT: MICHAL ZALEWSKI / WIKIMEDIA COMMONS

Carlos Manuel de Céspedes

Céspedes turned the "slave bell" into the bell of freedom

Céspedes was a Cuban lawyer and owner of a sugar mill and plantation in eastern Cuba. On the morning of October 10, 1868, Céspedes rang the bell which customarily called his slaves to begin their work day. When they gathered, he announced that they were henceforth free and invited them to join in rebellion against the Spanish government that ruled Cuba. Céspedes led that effort until he was deposed in 1873 and killed by Spanish troops in 1874. The Ten-Year War ended in 1878. Slaves who fought with the rebels remained free, but other slaves were not given freedom.

Carlos Manuel de Céspedes
CREDIT: ARCHIVAL

Two more wars for independence would be fought: The Little War (1879–1880) and the Cuban War of Independence (1895–1898). Cuba achieved independence from Spain in 1898 but immediately became a de facto colony of the United States until 1959 when Fidel Castro and his forces overthrew president Fulgencio Batista.

Henry Reeve

One of Cuba's most famous heroes, Henry Reeve, was an American

Henry Reeve was an American, born in Brooklyn in 1850. Hearing about the Cuban uprising against Spain in 1868, Reeve arrived in Cuba in 1869 as part of an expeditionary force. While landing, the expedition was ambushed by the Spanish Army, Many were killed. Reeve was wounded but survived. After a number of battles he was again wounded, and in the future had to be strapped to his horse in order to ride into battle.

Henry Reeve
CREDIT: ARCHIVAL

To the Cubans, Reeve was known as *"Enrique–el Americano"* or simply *"El Inglesito,"* He served seven years in the Cuban Army, participating in 400 battles, and rose through the ranks to become a Brigadier General. He died at the age of 27 by his own hand when surrounded by Spanish troops.

In 2005, when Cuba brought together 1,586 doctors and other medical workers to provide assistance (refused by the US government) to the United States after Hurricane Katrina, the Cubans named the medical group the "Henry Reeve International Contingent of Doctors Specialized in Disasters and Serious Epidemics" in honor of Reeve. (After more than one week, the US government dismissively spurned the offer—see p. 136)

José Martí

Cuba's greatest hero was a poet

No, it is not Fidel Castro or Che Guevara. It is José Martí, the Cuban equivalent of Thomas Paine, George Washington, and Walt Whitman rolled up into one. He was an inspirational poet considered the father of the Revolution and the visionary whose ideas led to present-day Cuba.[7]

José Martí
CREDIT: ARCHIVAL

Martí lived in New York City from 1880 to 1894, where he founded the Cuban Revolutionary Party in 1892 and wrote:

> "One just principle from the depths of a cave is more powerful than an army" —speaking about the power of diplomacy over war before the Spanish-American war, 1891

> "I am in daily danger of giving my life for my country and duty, for I understand that duty and have the courage to carry it out—the duty of preventing the United States from spreading through the Antilles as Cuba gains its independence, and from overpowering with that additional strength our lands of America. I have lived in the monster and I know its entrails; my sling is David's." —writing about possible annexation by the United States before the Spanish-American war, 1895.

---

[7] https://en.wikipedia.org/wiki/José_Marti

> "Valer, pero milliones de veces mas, la vida de un solo ser humano que todas las propiedades del hombre mas rico de la tierra."

> In English: "The life of a single human being is millions of times more valuable than all the possessions of the richest person on earth"

> "Patria es humanidad"
> ("Homeland is humanity")

> Based on: "My country is the world. My countrymen are mankind." From the masthead of William Lloyd Garrison's anti-slavery newspaper, The Liberator.

Martí was killed in battle on May 19, 1895 in the early days of the revolution of the Cuban people against Spain.

Spanish-American War

The *Maine* ("Remember the *Maine*") was probably not sunk by the Spanish

You may recall from US History class that the Americans went to war with Spain because in 1898 the Spanish had sunk the American battleship *Maine* in Havana harbor with the loss of 261 lives. This is probably not true, and quite possibly the American government knew it was not true, but the government had wanted a war with Spain to gain control of both Cuba and the Philippines, to re-unite psychologically the North and South, and to renew the American people's support of a strong military, which had faded after the devastation of the Civil War that had ended 33 years earlier.

Although the Americans went to war claiming that the Spanish had sunk the *Maine* ("Remember the *Maine!*"), there has never been agreement on the definite cause. There are many theories concerning the ship's explosion and one of the most plausible was determined by an investigation in 1974 headed by Admiral Hyman Rickover, the "Father of the Nuclear Navy." Rickover's team determined that there was "no plausible evidence of penetration from the outside." That is, it could not have been caused by a mine external to the ship.

Wreckage of the battleship Maine, Havana harbor
CREDIT: ARCHIVAL

Instead, Rickover's group believed the most plausible explanation was that coal in a bunker adjacent to the ammunition magazine had spontaneously combusted. The US Navy had switched from anthracite coal to the hotter burning bituminous coal, a coal which unlike anthracite *was* subject to spontaneous combustion, and which had led to explosions on other navy ships, nearly sinking several of them.

The Americans did not defeat the Spanish Army in Cuba

The Cubans had already all-but-defeated the nearly 200,000-man Spanish Army when the Americans showed up. In 1898, the Americans arrived just in time to spend one month fighting the Spanish—alongside the Cuban army— in what Cubans call the *Hispano-Cuban-American War.* The Americans took credit for the victory, and seized the island, which they thereafter controlled one way or another until 1959, usually through nominal Cuban governments. Not only did the Americans take credit for the defeat of the Spanish, they did not allow the Cubans to attend the surrender ceremonies. The all-white Spanish army did not wish to surrender to the mixed-race "rabble" of Cuban rebels, an army that reflected the racial makeup of the country, being nearly 60% black. Even 40% of the Cuban officers were black. [8]

---

[8] www.thedailybeast.com/newsweek/2008/03/24/a-splendid-war-s-shameful-side.html

Cuba for the Misinformed

The Americans, who also looked down on both the Cubans and on their own black military units—this was at a time of violent racism in the American South—kept the Cubans from the ceremony. They also disarmed and disbanded the Cuban army, while allowing the Spanish to keep their weapons and return to Spain.

Teddy Roosevelt did not lead the Rough Riders in a charge up San Juan Hill

He did, however, lead his troops up *Kettle Hill*, which like San Juan Hill was part of the San Juan Heights just outside Santiago de Cuba. When he reached the top he discovered that other American soldiers were already there, including black American "Buffalo Soldiers." When Roosevelt then started to head toward the actual San Juan Hill, he found that still other American units had already taken control of that particular hill.

"Roosevelt's Rough Riders" were the 1st United States Volunteer Cavalry Regiment, raised for the Spanish-American War and composed largely of Native Americans, college athletes, cowboys, and ranchers. Roosevelt was posthumously awarded the Medal of Honor in 2001 for his actions in Cuba.

The Spanish invented the modern concentration camp

The English term "concentration camp" comes from the Spanish *reconcentrados*, which was the name of the internment camps set up by the Spanish military in Cuba for civilians during the Ten Years' War (1868-1878.) More than 200,000 Cubans died of starvation and disease during this time.

Yellow Fever

A Cuban doctor discovered the cause of yellow fever

Although American Army surgeon Walter Reed is credited with discovering the cause of yellow fever, his team actually only *confirmed* the work of Cuban doctor and scientist Dr. Carlos Finlay, who theorized in 1881 and later proved that yellow fever was transmitted by mosquitoes and not by direct contact with other humans. Finlay's work led to the controlling of mosquito populations as the way to prevent the spread of yellow fever.

Carlos Finlay.
CREDIT: ARCHIVAL

Revolution

The 26th of July Movement was not the first revolt against a Cuban government, but it was the first truly successful one. It included not just Fidel Castro's forces in the mountains and countryside, but very active movements in the cities with large student participation.

The Americans initially continued to back Cuba's president Fulgencio Batista, but when they that saw his support was disappearing, in effect switched sides by no longer providing Batista with weapons and supplies. Castro's victory was very popular in the United States. Briefly. When the US government saw that he was serious about changing the structure of Cuban society and its economy, any popularity in Washington, D.C. was gone.

While the successful revolution had been a result of the support of the majority of Cubans, there is no doubt that the charismatic leaders of that revolution were critical to its success. Those leaders included the Castro brothers, Fidel and Raúl, as well as other commanders such as Camilo Cienfuegos and Che Guevara. Behind the scenes were many women, most notably Celia Sánchez and Vilma Espín, both of whom, along with the men, were responsible for Cuba's post-revolution accomplishments.

Timetable
Courtesy of Wikipedia

The Cuban Revolution culminated in the overthrow of the Batista regime by the 26th of July Movement and the establishment of a new Cuban government led by Fidel Castro in 1959. It began with an assault on the Moncada Barracks on July 26, 1953, and ended on January 1, 1959, when Batista was driven from the country after the cities of Santa Clara and Santiago de Cuba had been seized by rebels.

1953
July 26 – Some 160 revolutionaries under the command of Fidel Castro launch an attack on the Moncada barracks in Santiago de Cuba.

October 16 – Fidel Castro makes "History Will Absolve Me" speech in his own defense against the charges brought on him after the attack on the Moncada Barracks.

Cuba for the Misinformed

1954

September – Che Guevara arrives in Mexico City.

November – Fulgencio Batista dissolves parliament and is elected constitutional president without opposition.

1955

May – Fidel Castro and surviving members of his movement are released from prison under an amnesty from Batista.

June – Brothers Fidel and Raúl Castro are introduced to Che Guevara in Mexico City.

1956

November 25 – Fidel Castro, with some eighty insurgents, including Raúl Castro, Che Guevara and Camilo Cienfuegos, sets sail from Mexico for Cuba on the yacht *Granma*.

December 2 – *Granma* lands in Oriente Province.

1957

January 17 – Castro's guerrillas score their first success by sacking an army outpost on the south coast, and start gaining followers in both Cuba and abroad.

March 13 – University students mount an unsuccessful attack on the Presidential Palace in Havana.

May 28 – Castro's 26th of July Movement overwhelms an army post in El Uvero.

July 30 – Cuban revolutionary Frank País is killed in the streets of Santiago de Cuba by police while campaigning for the overthrow of Batista government.

1958

February – Raúl Castro opens a front in the Sierra de Cristal on Oriente's north coast.

March 13 – US suspends shipments of arms to Batista's forces.

March 17 – Fidel Castro calls for a general revolt.

April 9 – A general strike, organized by the 26th of July Movement, is partially observed.

May – Batista sends an army of 10,000 into the Sierra Maestra to destroy Castro's 300 armed guerrillas. By August, the rebels have defeated the army's advance and captured a huge amount of arms.

November 1 – A Cuban aircraft en route from Miami to Havana is hijacked by militants but crashes. The hijackers were trying to land at Sierra Cristal in Eastern Cuba to deliver weapons to Raúl Castro's rebels.

December 28-31 – Troops led by Che Guevara and Camilo Cienfuegos seize the city of Santa Clara.

1959

January 1 – Batista flees Cuba for the Dominican Republic. Fidel Castro's column enters Santiago de Cuba.

January 2 – Che Guevara and Camilo Cienfuegos enter Havana.

January 8 – Fidel Castro enters Havana.

Fulgencio Batista

Batista *was* elected president of Cuba—but not the *second* time he took office

President Fulgencio Batista of Cuba.
CREDIT: ARCHIVAL

Fulgencio Batista was an elected president of Cuba from 1940 to 1944. He had controlled Cuba since 1933 when he and others of the Cuban military overthrew president Gerardo Machado. Batista, as head of the military, effectively controlled a succession of Cuban presidents. After his term ended in 1944, he went to the United States but returned to run again for the presidency in 1950. When it became obvious that Batista would lose the election, he instead led a successful coup and installed himself as president of the Cuban republic.

Among Batista's greatest supporters was the American Mafia, which with his help controlled drugs, gambling and prostitution in Cuba. Batista's government matched any hotel investment over one million dollars—with a casino license included. This was an attractive offer to members of the Mob such as Meyer Lansky, who became the kingpin of the American presence in Havana. To Batista's credit, he also launched major construction projects, including the Havana-Varadero highway, the Rancho Boyeros airport, train lines, and an underwater tunnel. [9]

Batista's government murdered an estimated 20,000 Cubans in the years from 1952 through 1958.[10] His strong supporter the American government changed its mind when he started losing the civil war, and his request to seek safety at his home in Florida was refused.

After Fidel Castro and others of the rebellion were successful, Batista fled to the Dominican Republic with millions of dollars (some claim as much as 40-50 million). He eventually received asylum in Portugal and died in Spain in 1973.

Recommended viewing—

Cuba before Fidel Castro—http://youtu.be/8ILjG9VTIs4

July 26 Movement

The successful Cuban Revolution began with Fidel Castro's capture— and later release

The 26th of July Movement commemorates the 1953 attack on the Batista government's Moncada army barracks in Santiago de Cuba. More than seventy of the attackers were killed and others captured (and released in 1955). Those released included Fidel Castro and his brother Raúl, who both went into exile in Mexico. Fidel, along with Raúl, Che Guevara and seventy-nine other revolutionaries, returned to Cuba in 1956 and re-launched what became their successful revolution.

---

[9] http://www.pbs.org/wgbh/amex/castro/peopleevents/p_batista.html

[10] *Conflict, Order, and Peace in the Americas,* by the Lyndon B. Johnson School of Public Affairs, 1978, pg. 121

Interrogation of Fidel Castro after his capture in
Moncada Barracks raid.
CREDIT: ARCHIVAL

Recommended viewing—

Castro Triumphant! Revolt Success, Batista Flees
http://youtu.be/5Of4eA1N8Zw

Fidel Castro entering Havana—http://youtu.be/Y3BPfvJVf7s

Fidel Castro entering Havana (in Spanish)—http://youtu.be/HEvw6gcGgT8

Granma

The official newspaper in Cuba is named after the boat that launched the Revolution

The small yacht *Granma* was used by Fidel Castro and eighty-one others to sail from Mexico to Cuba, landing on December 2, 1956.

Most of the attacking force was killed or captured, but twelve began their campaign in the Sierra Maestra mountains in Oriente Province.

Cuba for the Misinformed

The yacht *Granma* used by Fidel Castro on his voyage from Mexico to Cuba.
CREDIT: ARCHIVAL

The boat is now on display at the Museum of the Revolution in Havana and its name is used for the official newspaper of the Central Committee of the Cuban Communist Party.

The newspaper *Granma* produces an online English version which can be seen at:

www. granma.cu/ingles

The *Granma* today, on display *at* the Museum of the Revolution, Havana.

American Guerrillas in Cuba

One of the top guerrilla leaders of the Cuban Revolution was an American

William Morgan was a US citizen who fought in the Cuban Revolution. He and Che Guevara (an Argentine) were the only two non-Cubans to reach the rank of Comandante in the revolutionary forces. Morgan was called the "*Yanquí Comandante.*"

William Morgan in the Sierra Cristal.
CREDIT: LATIN AMERICAN STUDIES.ORG

Morgan arrived in Cuba in 1957 and joined up in central Cuba with the Second National Front of the Escambray, a group that was strongly anti-communist and pro-democracy. His forces and those of Che Guevara and Camilo Cienfuegos captured the city of Santa Clara in a decisive battle in 1958, and Morgan's group soon after occupied the city of Cienfuegos.

After the revolutionary army had taken Cuba, Morgan supposedly helped foil an attempted coup organized by the Dominican Republic's leader Rafael Trujillo (along with the CIA). However, another version is that Morgan was involved with the plot all along and only exposed it *after* he knew that Fidel was already aware.

There is no doubt that Morgan was strongly anti-communist, and there was great animosity between him and Guevara, who was an ardent communist. As Cuba leaned more and more toward socialism and communism, Morgan's anti-communist attitude became suspect. He was arrested in October 1960 and charged with working with foreign interests to commit treason. His

41

Cuban wife—Olga Rodriguez—was also convicted. She eventually spent twelve years in a Cuban prison and later emigrated to the United States to live in Toledo, Ohio.

US government records released over the years show that, while US intelligence agencies were well aware of Morgan, there is no record that he was working with any of them. What he and his wife *had* done was to store weapons in the Escambray mountains as a precaution in case Morgan's strong anti-communist beliefs led to the need to escape into the mountains for safety. The Cuban government produced no evidence that Morgan was a US agent or was planning a coup. The act of storing the weapons should have been subject to a nine-year prison sentence, not to death. [11] On March 11, 1961, at the age of 32, he was executed by a firing squad at La Cabana prison in Havana.

The US government had taken away Morgan's US citizenship in 1959 because he served in a foreign government's military—something that the US government did *not* do to at least six other Americans who were with the Cuban guerrillas. In 2007, Morgan's citizenship was posthumously restored.

William Morgan was not the only American fighting with the anti-Batista guerrillas

Don Soldini was a 19-year-old kid from Brooklyn whose father was a Wobbly (member of the International Workers of the World union). He has said he would have fought in Spain with the Abraham Lincoln Brigade if it had been 1938. However, it was 1957, and when he found out about Castro, he made his way to Cuba and joined Raúl Castro's forces in the Sierra Cristal. Returning to the United States after the rebel victory, Soldini eventually started a career as a Fort Lauderdale-based developer of international resorts. [12] [13]

Neil Macaulay was a graduate of the Citadel military school and had been a first lieutenant in the US Army in post-war Korea. In September 1958, at the age of 23, he joined up with the anti-Batista guerrillas in Pinar del Rio Province, west of Havana. On January 1, 1959, the day after Batista left Cuba, Macaulay submitted his resignation. It was not accepted and instead he was promoted to first lieutenant and sent after Batista holdouts in the area. He was then put in charge of training a firing squad in Pinar del Rio to deal with men who had committed crimes under Batista. After the initial eleven executions, it was clear to him that the men he had trained could do fine without him, and he left the army in March to raise tomatoes in central Cuba.

---

[11] Toledo Blade http://bit.ly/So0HNK

[12] StAugustine.com http://bit.ly/SjlMZw

[13] Miami Herald www2.fiu.edu/~fcf/yanquifidelistas.html

As a result of lessening democracy and increasing anti-business and anti-American sentiments in Cuba, he and his American wife left the country in July 1960 and returned to the States, with Macaulay going to graduate school and later becoming a professor of Latin American History in Florida. [14]

Charles Ryan (19), **Victor J. Buehlman** (17) and **Michael L. Garvey** (15) were all teenagers living at the US naval base in Guantánamo, where their fathers were members of the US Navy. In March 1957, the three sneaked away from Guantánamo and joined the rebels in the mountains.

After a report by Herbert Matthews on Fidel Castro appeared in the *New York Times*, CBS producer Robert Taber and cameraman Wendell Hoffman went to the Sierra Maestra in April and filmed a documentary titled *Rebels of the Sierra Maestra: The Story of Cuba's Jungle Fighters*. Part of that film was a long interview with the three American teenagers. [15] The two younger ones, Buehlman and Garvey, who had mainly been doing guard duty, returned to Guantánamo with Taber—Castro was worried about bad publicity if an American teenager were killed—and were immediately shipped back to the States. Ryan remained with Castro's forces, serving under Fidel's brother Raúl. [16]

In October 1957, Castro sent Ryan to the United States to raise funds and buy guns for the rebels. Afterwards Ryan joined the US Army for a career as a paratrooper. [17] Buehlman later became a sales manager for an electrical equipment company in Tennessee. Garvey also spent time in the US military.

New York Times

Fidel Castro's small group of guerrillas in the Sierra Maestra looked much bigger in the *New York Times*

In February 1957, Castro and his rebels were visited by the *Times* reporter Herbert Matthews. This was at a time when the rebels were in the mountains of the Sierra Maestra and Fulgencio Batista was telling the people of Cuba and the world that Castro had been killed two months earlier.

---

[14] American Heritage www.americanheritage.com/content/i-fought-fidel

[15] "You guys got us $5,000,000 worth of publicity for that," Castro told Ryan. "We couldn't have paid an ad agency for that." Jonathan M. Hansen, Guantánamo: An American History, p.214

[16] www.historyofcuba.com/history/havana/Fidel-2.htm

[17] StAugustine.com http://bit.ly/SjlMZw

Cuba for the Misinformed

New York Times correspondent Herbert Matthews with
Fidel Castro.
CREDIT: H.L. MATTHEWS PAPERS, RARE BOOK AND MANUSCRIPT LIBRARY,
COLUMBIA UNIVERSITY

Matthews proved this untrue when he brought back a photograph of Castro.
As Che Guevara later wrote, "...when the world had given us up for dead, the
interview with Matthews put the lie to our disappearance." [18]

Even more impressive was Matthews' report of the large numbers of Castro's
forces. As Georgie Ann Geyer writes in her book *Guerrilla Prince: The Untold
Story of Fidel Castro.* [19]

> Fidel staged one of the most extraordinary shows of Sierra
> history, which some have rightly called "guerrilla theater." For
> his part, Matthews thought he counted approximately forty
> fighters where there were no more than twenty, and he was
> convinced that a much larger force hovered hungrily in the
> high jungles.
>
> Actually it was all quite simple. Fidel had instructed his men to
> "adopt martial airs." One by one, then two by two, they
> marched by Matthews. Then they marched by him again, and
> again, and again. (One man had no back to his shirt and had to
> march sideways.) Raúl even brought one exhausted man, Luis
> Crespo, over to Fidel and Matthews, reporting smartly,
> "Comandante, the liaison from Column Number 2 has
> arrived," to which Fidel haughtily replied, "Wait until I'm
> finished."

---

[18] www.hartford-hwp.com/archives/43b/066.html

[19] Georgie Anne Geyer, *Guerrilla Prince: The Untold Story of Fidel Castro,* Little, Brown and
Company (1991)

As Che Guevara later said, "At that time the presence of a foreign journalist—preferably from the United States—was more important to us than a military victory. It was more important to have US combatants who would help export our revolutionary propaganda than to recruit to the struggle peasants who were bringing to the revolution their ideals and their faith ." [20]

In the United States, the conservative magazine *National Review* agreed. One issue had a caricature of Fidel Castro with the caption—itself a phrase used by the *Times* to promote its classified advertising—"I got my job through the *New York Times.*" [21]

Radio Rebelde

Rebel Radio has been broadcasting music and revolution since 1958

On February 24, 1958, Ché Guevara set up *Radio Rebelde* (Rebel Radio – "The voice of the Sierra Maestra") transmitting from his rebel camp deep in the heart of the Sierra Maestra mountains in eastern Cuba. The first transmission lasted only twenty minutes, but the station has continued to broadcast ever since (www.radiorebelde.com.cu).

Radio Rebelde logo.
CREDIT: RADIO REBELDE

Alberto Korda

Alberto Korda received no payment for his iconic photograph of Che Guevara

Cuban photographer Alberto Korda (1928-2001) never received any payment or royalties for what is often considered the best-known and most reproduced photograph in the world.

---

[20] www.themilitant.com/1999/6311/6311_25.html

[21] National Review Online http://bit.ly/RXtHtV

Famous (and cropped) photo of
Che Guevara.
CREDIT: ALBERTO KORDA

Korda took the photograph on March 5, 1960, the day after the French ship *La Coubre* exploded in Havana's harbor, loaded with munitions for the revolutionary government. More than 75 people were killed. Guevara, who had personally provided medical treatment to the victims, was among the crowd at a memorial march, and Korda snapped just two shots of him.

Some years later Korda gave two prints of the photo to Italian publisher Giangiacomo Feltrinelli who distributed posters of the image and also used it after Che's execution on the cover of Che's *Bolivian Diary* when it was published in 1968. Korda did not charge Feltrinelli for the use of the prints, nor did Feltrinelli, who made a fortune from selling and licensing use of the print, ever give Korda any payment. [22]   Korda said, "If he had paid me just one lira for each reproduction, we would have received millions, but I still forgive him, because by doing what he did he made it famous." [23]

---

[22] Times of London   http://bit.ly/So0wSM

[23] Times of London   http://bit.ly/So0wSM

Original *uncropped* photo of Che Guevara.
CREDIT: ALBERTO KORDA

In 2000 Korda sued Smirnoff in London for using the image of Che in an advertisement. Korda told the Guardian newspaper: "To use the image of Che Guevara to sell vodka is a slur on his name and memory." More officially, Korda stated:

> As a supporter of the ideals for which Che Guevara died, I am not averse to its reproduction by those who wish to propagate his memory and the cause of social justice throughout the world, but I am categorically against the exploitation of Che's image for the promotion of products such as alcohol, or for any purpose that denigrates the reputation of Che. [24]

Korda donated his out-of-court settlement (said to be US $50,000) for Cuban healthcare, saying, "If Che were still alive, he would have done the same."

---

[24] http://news.bbc.co.uk/2/hi/americas/1352650.stm

Cuba for the Misinformed

Alberto Korda
CREDIT: CUBARTE

La niña con la muñeca de palo
(The girl with the stick doll)
CREDIT: ALBERTO KORDA

Nearing 30, I was heading toward a frivolous life when an exceptional event transformed my life: The Cuban Revolution. It was at this time that I took this photo of a little girl, who was clutching a piece of wood for a doll. I came to understand that it was worth dedicating my work to a revolution which aimed to remove these inequalities. - Alberto Korda

Recommended viewing—

Simply Korda—A documentary on Cuban photographer Alberto Korda
www.havana-cultura.com/en/nl/visual-art/photographer/alberto-korda

Errol Flynn

Movie star Errol Flynn filmed *Cuban Rebel Girls* with Fidel Castro's cooperation during the revolution

Australian-born Errol Flynn, swashbuckling star of American movies in the 1930s and 1940s such as "Captain Blood," and "The Adventures of Robin Hood," spent considerable time enjoying the pre-Revolution delights of Havana—casinos and brothels. However, he also ended up on a trip to the Sierra Maestra, [25] ostensibly as a reporter for Hearst newspapers, for whom he wrote a series of articles on Castro and the 26th of July Movement. [26]

Errol Flynn (in white shirt) at meeting with Fidel Castro (bottom center.
CREDIT: ARCHIVAL

Flynn made two films about Cuba, one of them considered to be in the running for the worst movie ever made. That was *Cuban Rebel Girls*, also known as *Assault of the Rebel Girls*, which was made with Castro's cooperation. The film starred Flynn's teenage girlfriend Beverly Aadland and Flynn playing himself as a war correspondent. The second, completed after Flynn's death later the same year (1959), was a documentary entitled *The Truth about Fidel Castro Revolution,* later changed to *Cuban Story.* This film includes both important historical footage and scenes of Flynn not at his best as he attempts to discuss the Cuban Revolution.

---

[25] www.cbc.ca/archives/discover/great-interviews/revolution-in-cuba.html

[26] Sarasota Journal   http://bit.ly/So2Uce

Santa Clara

A bulldozer helped bring victory to the Cuban Revolution

Santa Clara, located in the central part of Cuba, is the site of the last battle of the Cuban Revolution. Over the period of December 28 to 31, 1958, 300 men led by Che Guevara and Camilo Cienfuegos attacked 3,000 government and local force equipped with tanks, armored cars, and numerous light and heavy weapons. The rebels used a bulldozer to destroy railroad tracks and derail a troop and supply train. The rebels seized bazookas, machine guns, mortars, a 20mm cannon, 600 rifles and approximately one million rounds of ammunition, while taking 350 prisoners. The engagement, the biggest of the revolution, was a decisive action that resulted in the capture of the city and led to Batista fleeing the island twelve hours later. [27]

Guevara's remains are interred in a monument in Santa Clara, along with the remains of sixteen other colleagues who were also killed in Bolivia.

Recommended viewing—

Che Guevara Mausoleum/Railroad Museum
http://youtu.be/CDvSiTaUda0

Close up of Che Guevara monument
CREDIT: BLUESYPETE/WIKIMEDIA COMMONS

---

[27] http://latinamericanhistory.about.com/od/historyofthecaribbean/a/08battlestaclar.htm

Museum of the Revolution

Tourists can see the engine of the American spy plane that Soviets shot down during the Cuban Missile Crisis

The Museum of the Revolution was established by Celia Sánchez in 1959 in what had been Fulgencio Batista's presidential palace, originally opened in 1920. Key exhibits include the *Granma,* the boat that Fidel Castro and seventy-nine others used in 1956 to travel from Mexico to Cuba to begin the revolution, and the engine from the Lockheed U-2 spy plane shot down by a Soviet surface-to-air missile during the Cuban Missile Crisis.

The museum also displays the space suit worn by Arnaldo Tamayo Méndez, the first Cuban, first Hispanic and first black person in space, who was aboard the Soviet Union's *Soyuz 38* on its space flight in 1980.

Recommended viewing—

Museum of the Revolution—http://youtu.be/aNMrHu1mgKc

Museum of the Revolution—http://youtu.be/3xAZWtywMQY

Camilo Cienfuegos

One of the leaders of the revolution disappeared on a flight over the ocean ten months after victory

Camilo Cienfuegos first met Fidel Castro in Mexico, then sailed with Castro on the *Granma* to Cuba at the start of the revolution. Cienfuegos was later promoted to Comandante in 1957 and was for a time head of the Cuban armed forces once the revolution was over.

Camilo Cienfuegos (right) with Fidel Castro.
CREDIT: ARCHIVAL

Cienfuegos' forces had been victorious at the Battle of Yaguajay in December 1958, and he then joined forces with Che Guevara and a column led by William Morgan to capture the town of Santa Clara, resulting in Batista's flight from the country and the successful end of the revolution.

Cienfuegos' aircraft disappeared over the ocean on October 28, 1959, on a night flight from Camaguey to Havana. A search was unsuccessful and no traces of the aircraft or its passengers were ever found.

Every October 28 children throughout Cuba throw flowers into the sea in honor of Cienfuegos. As the children throw the flowers into the sea (or a river if they are inland), they say, "*una flor por Camilo*" (a flower for Camilo).

Camilo Cienfuegos
CREDIT: ARCHIVAL

Fifty years after his death, Camilo Cienfuegos' face joined that of Che Guevara in Havana's Plaza of the Revolution

The 100-ton steel outline can now be seen on the side of the Ministry of Informatics and Communications. Along with the image are the words *Vas bien, Fidel* ("You're doing fine, Fidel") referring to a famous incident in 1959 when Fidel Castro was speaking to a large crowd and declared that a military barracks would be turned into a school. Then he turned to Cienfuegos and asked "Am I doing all right, Camilo?"

Image of Camilo Cienfuegos on Ministry of Informatics and Communication, Havana
CREDIT: CARLOS REUSSER MONSALVEZ/FLICKR

Recommended viewing—

Camilo Cienfuegos Gorriaran. A portrait of a revolutionary
http://youtu.be/ViZkrP7TPFU

Celia Sánchez

Celia Sánchez is considered to have been the most powerful woman in Revolutionary Cuba

Celia Sánchez
CREDIT: ARCHIVAL

Sánchez was among the first to take action against the government of Fulgencio Batista after he took power in a coup on March 10, 1952. While Castro was forming what he called The Movement in the Havana area, Sánchez was organizing a resistance movement in eastern Cuba.

Sánchez and Castro did not meet until February 1957 in the Sierra Maestra when she was coordinating weapons, supplies and communications for the rebel forces. She became, and remained, Castro's closest female friend—and quite likely lover—until she died in 1980.

Sánchez served as an unofficial historian from the beginning of the revolution, saving every note, letter, report and other artifacts for the eventual Office of Historical Affairs and Museum of the Revolution, both of which she established. She also created the famous ice cream parlor *Coppelia* in Havana, reportedly named after her favorite ballet. Sánchez wanted the ice cream parlor to be a meeting place for young and old, students and professionals, blacks, whites and mulattos,[28] Sánchez also established Lenin Park, nearly three square miles (1878 acres) on the southern edge of Havana. It offers an amusement park, lake, bicycle riding, swimming pools, shops, bars, an aquarium and restaurants.

Sánchez even named Cuba's most famous cigar, originally created only for Fidel Castro, other top members of the government, and distinguished visitors. *Cohiba* cigars can now be purchased by everyone—except Americans, of course. Their name comes from the Taino Indian word for a roll of dry tobacco leaves, which are lit and smoked as part of a religious ritual..[29]

Recommended viewing—

Celia Sánchez (in Spanish)—http://youtu.be/RnXxnvl_QSA

In memory of Celia Sánchez—http://youtu.be/058CusQ2CKY

Che Guevara

A tribute to Ernesto "Che" Guevara

> Che died defending no other interest, no other cause than the cause of the exploited and the oppressed of this continent. Che died defending no other cause than the cause of the poor and the humble of this earth. And the exemplary manner and the selflessness with which he defended that cause cannot be disputed by even his most bitter enemies.
>
> —Fidel Castro, October 18, 1967

---

[28] http://www.csmonitor.com/1998/0625/062598.intl.intl.4.html   http://bit.ly/YBe69l

[29] http://cigars.co.uk/blog/cohiba-behike-brief-history?accept=1   http://bit.ly/Vn7U69

Che Guevara at age 22
CREDIT: ERNESTO GUEVARA LYNCH/WIKIMEDIA COMMONS

Che Guevara
CREDIT: ALBERTO KORDA

Che Guevara
CREDIT: ALBERTO KORDA

Che's goal was creation of the "New Man"

Guevara felt that the attitudes in Cuba towards race, women, individualism, and manual labor were the result of the country's outdated past. He urged everyone to take on the values of *el Hombre Nuevo* (the "New Man"). He saw that the New Man would be "selfless and cooperative, obedient and hard-working, gender-blind, incorruptible, non-materialistic, and anti-imperialist. He saw socialism as the route to this new individual and thought that the state should emphasize egalitarianism and self-sacrifice, "unity, equality, and freedom."

He believed, "Man truly achieves his full human condition when he produces without being compelled by the physical necessity of selling himself as a commodity." [30] He viewed capitalism as a "contest among wolves" where "one can only win at the cost of others."

As Guevara stated,

> There is a great difference between free-enterprise development and revolutionary development. In one of them, wealth is concentrated in the hands of a fortunate few, the friends of the

---

[30] http://www.marxists.org/archive/guevara/1965/03/man-socialism-alt.htm

government, the best wheeler-dealers. In the other, wealth is the people's patrimony. [31]

Guevara controlled the Cuban economy with his positions of Finance Minister, President of the National Bank, and Minister of Industries. His first step in his desired direction, as head of the bank, was to sign the currency, which he did; not with his full name but simply with "Che." This horrified Cuba's financial sector but made clear Guevara's contempt for money.

Che Guevara was, and is, loved and worshipped, despised and reviled by people all over the world. Here are some views of Guevara from the Wikipedia section on Che Guevara. [32]

> Nelson Mandela referred to him as "an inspiration for every human being who loves freedom," while Jean-Paul Sartre described him (Guevara, incidentally, spoke fluent French) as "not only an intellectual but also the most complete human being of our age." Author Graham Greene remarked that Che "represented the idea of gallantry, chivalry, and adventure", and Susan Sontag expounded that "[Che's] goal was nothing less than the cause of humanity itself."

> Philosopher Frantz Fanon professed Guevara to be "the world symbol of the possibilities of one man", while Black Panther Party head Stokely Carmichael eulogized that "Che Guevara is not dead, his ideas are with us." Libertarian theorist Murray Rothbard extolled Guevara as a "heroic figure", lamenting after his death that "more than any man of our epoch or even of our century, [Che] was the living embodiment of the principle of revolution."

> Jacobo Machover, an exiled opposition author, portrayed Guevara as a ruthless executioner. Former Cuban prisoer Armando Valladares echoed similar sentiments, declaring Che "a man full of hatred" while accusing him of executing dozens who never stood trial.

Detractors theorized that Che-inspired revolutions in much of Latin America reinforced brutal militarism and internecine conflict for many years. British historian Hugh Thomas opined that Che was a "brave, sincere and determined man who was also obstinate, narrow, and dogmatic." At the end of his life, according to Thomas, "he seems to have become convinced of the virtues of violence for its own sake", while "his influence over Castro for good or evil" grew after his death, as Fidel took up many of his views.

---

[31] Douglas Kellner (1989), *Ernesto "Che" Guevara (World Leaders Past & Present)*. Chelsea House Publishers, p. 59.

[32] http://en.wikipedia.org/wiki/Che_Guevara

Cuba for the Misinformed

Quotations from Che Guevara

I am Cuban, Argentine, Bolivian, Peruvian, Ecuadorian, etc... You understand. (when asked his nationality)

The revolution is not an apple that falls when it is ripe. You have to make it fall.

We cannot be sure of having something to live for unless we are willing to die for it.

Whenever death may surprise us, let it be welcome if our battle cry has reached even one receptive ear and another hand reaches out to take up our arms.

I am not a liberator. Liberators do not exist. The people liberate themselves.

I know you are here to kill me. Shoot, coward, you are only going to kill a man.

Recommended viewing—

Che Guevara interview in Ireland 1964—http://youtu.be/vBYUOOOEHbJw

Che Guevara speaks to United Nations 1964 (in Spanish) http://youtu.be/bufHojkoGtw

English translation—http://youtu.be/a8po84osCl8

English subtitles—http://youtu.be/-ekfej_kmHQ

The true story of Che Guevara – a Documentary http://youtu.be/g-ZJAS_ZzKU

Since Che Guevara's death, he has been presented as the model for all Cubans, particularly children

Near the end of Fidel Castro's tribute at Che Guevara's memorial, Castro launched the iconic future of Guevara:

...If we want to tell how we hope our revolutionary fighters, our militants, our men should be, we should say without hesitation that they should be like CHE;

...if we want to tell how we want the men of future generations to be, we should say they should be like CHE;

... if we want to say how we want our children to be educated, we should say without hesitation they should be reared in the spirit of CHE, if we want a pattern of a man, a pattern of a man that does not belong to this time, but to future times, from the bottom of my heart I say that pattern with not a stain in his behavior, not a stain in his attitude, nor in his actions, that pattern is CHE;

...if we want to know how we want our children to be, we should say from the bottom of our heart we want them to be like CHE. If we want to tell how we hope our revolutionary fighters, our militants, our men should be, we should say without hesitation that they should be like CHE;

...if we want to tell how we want the men of future generations to be, we should say they should be like CHE; if we want to say how we want our children to be educated, we should say without hesitation they should be reared in the spirit of CHE, if we want a pattern of a man, a pattern of a man that does not belong to this time, but to future times, from the bottom of my heart I say that pattern with not a stain in his behavior, not a stain in his attitude, nor in his actions, that pattern is CHE;

...if we want to know how we want our children to be, we should say from the bottom of our heart we want them to be like CHE." [33]

Che's remains were discovered in Bolivia thirty years after his death and returned to Cuba

In 1997, Cuban and Argentinian forensic teams discovered the remains of Che Guevara in Bolivia. They had already found the remains of some of his comrades the previous year. Guevara had been executed in 1967 and his body buried at a landing strip outside the town of Vallegrande, where his body had been displayed at a hospital for the press and others. The skeletons of Che and six others were exhumed and examined over a period of ten days or so. During the process, to ensure the security of the remains, members of the team slept in the grave and later in the hospital morgue where the remains had been taken.

---

[33] www.companeroche.com/index.php?id=105

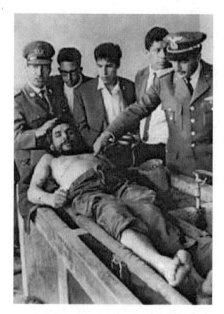

Che Guevara shortly after his murder.
CREDIT: FREDDY ALBORTA

The remains were positively identified with a wide variety of forensic tests, then flown back to Cuba. On October 17, 1997 they were entombed in a special memorial in the city of Santa Clara, where Che's military victory had led to Fulgencio Batista's fleeing the country.

The man who killed Che had his eyesight restored years later by Cuban doctors

Che Guevara was shot and killed by a Bolivian army sergeant, Mario Terán, who had been ordered to execute Guevara. In 2006—39 years later—the former sergeant was given free eye surgery by Cuban doctors who treated his cataract condition and restored his eyesight. The surgery was part of a free program conducted by Cuban doctors throughout Latin America. The Cubans were apparently unaware of who he was at the time because Terán used a false name.

Che Guevara disguised in 1966
as Uruguyan businessman
Adolfo Mena González
in order to enter Bolivia.
CREDIT: ANONYMOUS / WIKIMEDIA COMMONS

A Cuban-American CIA officer kept some mementos from Che Guevara's death

Felix Rodriguez oversaw the capture and execution of Che Guevara. Rodriguez took, and still proudly wears, one of the Rolex watches that Guevara had in his possession. [34]

As Rodriguez wrote twenty-five years later, he also acquired another souvenir:

> "Che may have been dead, but somehow his asthma—a condition that I never had in my life—had attached itself to me. To this day, my chronic shortness of breath is a constant reminder of Che and his last hours alive in the tiny town of La Higuera." [35]

Recommended reading—

The Death of Che Guevara: Declassified
www.gwu.edu/~nsarchiv/NSAEBB/NSAEBB5/

---

[34] Watchfinder http://bit.ly/X954lN

[35] Jon Lee Anderson, *Che Guevara: A Revolutionary Life*, p. 741

Che's visage looks down on the mammoth Plaza de la Revolución in Havana

A steel sculpture of Che Guevara's image is on the side of the Ministry of the Interior headquarters in Havana, a building which once housed the Ministry of Industries headed by Guevara.

The image is a replica of the famous photograph by Alberto Korda. The words below are Guevara's well-known phrase: *Hasta la Victoria Siempre* ("Onward to victory").

Che Guevara image on the Ministry of the Interior, Havana
CREDIT: MARK SCOTT JOHNSON/WIKIMEDIA COMMONS

Fidel Castro

Fidel Castro led his country while ten US presidents came and went

Castro was the leader of Cuba during the terms of ten US presidents, starting with Dwight Eisenhower, and ending when Castro retired during the presidency of George W. Bush. Today Castro still remains very influential, while the United States is on yet another president, Barack Obama.

Fidel Castro (2003)
CREDIT: ANTONIO MILENA— ABR/WIKIMEDIA COMMONS

Until Castro officially retired as president in 2008, he was the world's third-longest serving current head of state. Bhumibol Adulyadej of Thailand is the world's longest-serving current head of state, since 1946, and Queen Elizabeth of the UK is in second place, having reigned since 1952.

Fidel Castro (right) with Camilo Cienfuegos as they
enter Havana on 8 January 1959
CREDIT: LUIS KORDA (LUIS PIERCE)

Castro and his first wife spent a three-month honeymoon in the United States

In 1948 Castro married Mirta Díaz Balart, a member of a wealthy Cuban
family with close ties to the government. Mirta's father was a lawyer with the
United Fruit Company and mayor of United Fruit's company town,
interestingly, the birthplace of Fulgencio Batista). [36]

---

[36] www.pbs.org/wgbh/amex/castro/peopleevents/p_castro.html

Fidel Castro and his first wife Mirta Díaz Balart.
CREDIT: ARCHIVAL

Mirta's father gave them thousands of dollars for a three-month long honeymoon in Miami and New York City. Her father wasn't the only one who helped out with the costs of the honeymoon. Another man, a military general and former president of Cuba, reportedly gave them a wedding gift of $1,000 for the honeymoon. (Another report said he was cheap and actually gave them only a table lamp). He was the man whom Castro would ten years later force out of office and out of the country, Fulgencio Batista.

Castro once held the record for the longest speech ever given at the United Nations

On September 29, 1960, Castro spoke to the United Nations General Assembly for four hours and twenty-nine minutes. Although that remains the longest General Assembly speech, Indian UN envoy Krishna Menon gave a record-breaking speech to the UN Security Council in 1957. Menon's speech, spread out over two days, lasted more than eight hours. (Menon collapsed from exhaustion part way through the speech. He was hospitalized but returned later and continued speaking while a doctor monitored his blood pressure.)

The longest speech on record by Castro in any location was seven hours and ten minutes at the Third Communist Party Congress in Havana in 1986.

Fidel Castro expropriated his own family farm

Fidel Castro, along with his brother Raúl and other siblings, grew up on a 26,000-acre plantation at the base of the Sierra Cristal mountains in eastern Cuba. More than just a large farm, it was an entire community. It included a country store, school house, post office, small restaurant, butcher shop, infirmary, and living quarters for the 400 family members and employees.

Cuba for the Misinformed

The farm produced sugar-cane, oranges, lumber and cattle, as well as enough food to feed everyone.

While Fidel and Raúl were off fighting, their brother Ramon looked after the farm. However, Ramon's role was critical to the revolution. He was, in effect, the quartermaster for Fidel's forces, providing food, supplies and vital information to the guerrillas.

In 1961, the new Cuban government began expropriating land owned by foreigners and wealthy Cubans. The Castro family farm was one of the first to go. "With one signature, Fidel took it all away," Ramon said, explaining that his brother had to demonstrate that *everyone's* lands would be taken over by the state—not just those belonging to enemies of the revolution. [37]

Fidel Castro kept his "campaign" promises

After Castro's failed attack on the Moncada barracks on July 26, 1953, he was captured and imprisoned. Many of his comrades had been summarily executed, but Castro two months later stood trial for the attack. At the trial on October 16, 1953, Castro gave his famous four-hour speech ending with "Condemn me. It does not matter. History will absolve me." [38] In this speech he listed the five revolutionary laws which his government would initiate. Castro and others, including his brother Raúl, were sentenced to prison. Two years later Batista granted them amnesty, and they were released.

The five "revolutionary laws" were:

- The reinstatement of the 1940 Cuban constitution and power returned to the people.
- A reformation of land rights giving ownership to all tenant and subtenant farmers, lessees, sharecroppers and squatters who held parcels of five *caballerias* or less. A caballeria is 33 acres (13 hectares). Former owners would be indemnified on the basis of the rent they would have received over ten years.
- The granting to workers and employees the right to share 30 percent of the profits of all large industrial, mercantile and mining enterprises, including sugar mills. Strictly agricultural enterprises would be dealt with separately.
- The granting to all sugar planters the right to share 55 percent of sugar production and a minimum quota of 40,000 *arrobas* for all small tenant farmers who had been established for three years or more. (An arroba is approximately four gallons or sixteen liters.)

---

[37] Herald Tribune   http://bit.ly/YmidqB

[38] www.marxists.org/history/cuba/archive/castro/1953/10/16.htm

- The confiscation of all "holdings and ill-gotten gains" of those who had committed frauds during previous regimes, as well as those of their legates and heirs. Half of the property recovered would be used to subsidize retirement funds for workers and the other half would be used for hospitals, asylums and charitable organizations.

These laws would be followed by additional laws and measures dealing with agrarian reform, educational reform, nationalization of electric power and telephone systems, refunds to the people of the illegal rates charged by those companies, and payment to the treasury of all taxes evaded by those companies in the past.

The new government would also initiate steps to solve the following six problems:

- Land
- Industrialization
- Housing
- Unemployment
- Education
- People's health

As you can read throughout this book, all of these problems have been, and continue to be, addressed by the Castro government.

Note: The speech, and its written record, also stated that a Castro government would restore "civil liberties and political democracy." Their actions in this area are less obvious and subject to discussion and disagreement.

In 1979, Castro spoke to the United Nations General Assembly on the worldwide gap between rich and poor

> There is often talk of human rights, but it is also necessary to speak of the rights of humanity. Why should some people walk around barefoot, so that others can travel in luxurious automobiles? Why should some live for thirty-five years, so that others can live for seventy? Why should some be miserably poor, so that others can be overly rich? I speak in the name of the children in the world who do not have a piece of bread. I speak in the name of the sick who do not have medicine. I speak on behalf of those whose right to life and human dignity have been denied. [39]

---

[39] Latin American Network Information Center   http://bit.ly/Usebbc

"Fight against the impossible and overcome"
CREDIT: JIM/WIKIMEDIA COMMONS

Castro's guerrillas became known as "*los barbudos*" (the bearded ones)

Castro stated in his book *My Life: A Spoken Autobiography*:

> The story of our beards is very simple: it arose out of the difficult conditions we were living and fighting under as guerrillas. We didn't have any razor blades... everybody just let their beards and hair grow, and that turned into a kind of badge of identity. For the campesinos and everybody else, for the press, for the reporters we were "los barbudos" - the bearded ones. It had its positive side: in order for a spy to infiltrate us, he had to start preparing months ahead of time - he'd have had to have six-months' growth of beard, you see... Later, with the triumph of the Revolution, we kept our beards to preserve the symbolism. [40]

Canada's prime minister and Fidel Castro were close friends

Pierre Elliott Trudeau, when prime minister of Canada, became not just a fellow leader of government but close friends with Fidel Castro.

As Trudeau's son Alexandre wrote on Castro's 80th birthday...

> "His [Fidel's] intellect is one of the most broad and complete that can be found. He is an expert on genetics, on automobile combustion engines, on stock markets. On everything.

---

[40] Fidel Castro, Ignacio Ramonet (interviewer) (2009). *My Life: A Spoken Autobiography.* New York: Scribner, p. 195.

He is something of a superman. My father once told us how he had expressed to Fidel his desire to do some diving in Cuba. Fidel took him to the most enchanting spot on the island and set him up with equipment and a tank. He stood back as my father geared up and began to dive alone.

When my father had reached a depth of around 60 feet, he realized that Fidel was down there with him, that he had descended without a tank and that there he was with a knife in hand prying sea urchins off the ocean floor, grinning." [41]

Fidel Castro and Canadian Prime Minister Pierre Trudeau
CREDIT: DUNCAN CAMERON/NATIONAL ARCHIVES OF CANADA

Quotations from Fidel Castro

A revolution is a struggle between the past and the future.

If there ever was in the history of humanity an enemy who was truly universal, an enemy whose acts and moves trouble the entire world, threaten the entire world, attack the entire world in any way or another, that real and really universal enemy is precisely Yankee imperialism.

If Mr. Kennedy does not like socialism, we do not like imperialism. We do not like capitalism. We have as much right to complain about the existence of a capitalist imperialist regime 90 miles from our coast as he has to complain about a socialist regime 90 miles from his coast.

---

[41] http://www.freerepublic.com/focus/f-news/1684552/posts

They talk about the failure of socialism but where is the success of capitalism in Africa, Asia and Latin America?

As I have said before, the ever more sophisticated weapons piling up in the arsenals of the wealthiest and the mightiest can kill the illiterate, the ill, the poor and the hungry, but they cannot kill ignorance, illness, poverty or hunger.

North Americans don't understand... that our country is not just Cuba; our country is also humanity.

In June 1958, the home of "Mario," a peasant friend of Fidel Castro, was destroyed by bombs from a Batista air force plane provided by the US. Mario had not been involved in the revolution. Castro was furious, and wrote the following short note to Celia Sánchez. [42]

Sierra Maestra
Junio 5-58
Celia:
Al ver los cohetes que tiraron en casa de Mario, me he jurado que los americanos van a pagar bien caro lo que están haciendo. Cuando esta guerra se acabe, empezará para mi una guerra mucho más larga y grande: la guerra que voy a echar contra ellos. Me doy cuenta que ese va a ser mi destino verdadero.
Fidel

Sierra Maestra
June 5-58
Celía:
At seeing the rockets fired at the house of Mario, I have sworn to myself that the Americans are going to pay dearly for what they are doing. When this war ends, for me will begin a much longer and bigger war: the war that I am going to wage against them. I realize that that will be my true destiny.
Fidel

Recommended viewing—

Viva Cuba: Fidel Castro and Pierre Trudeau
Part 1 - http://youtu.be/5eueOLhynoM
Part 2 - http://youtu.be/3K-C1sG-hbY

---

[42] http://www.latinamericanstudies.org/fidel/carta-fidel-celia.jpg

Nelson Mandela is a strong admirer of Fidel Castro

In his autobiography *Conservations with Myself* (2010), Nelson Mandela said about Fidel Castro:

> Castro is a very striking chap . . . We addressed a meeting together. What is the name of that town, man? A crowd like that in a small country? It was a fantastic crowd; I think there were about 300,000 people. Everyone seated on chairs. He spoke about three hours without a piece of paper, quoted figures, and he showed that America was bankrupt, you know? And not a single person left except to go to the toilet and come back .. . I was tremendously impressed by Castro and also by his humility – very humble chap, you know? When . . . I [was] driving with him through the city, he just sat down and folded his arms, and I was the person who was waving to the crowd . . . After speaking, we . . . went into the crowd; he was greeting everybody . . . I noticed that he will greet . . . a white person, then he goes to greet somebody who's dark. I don't know whether that was purely accidental or deliberate. [He was] very warm, talked to them for some time . . . I then realised that this enthusiasm and waving was not really for me as we were driving through the city; it was directed to Castro . . . Nobody bothered about me at all [laughs] . . . I was tremendously impressed by him. [43]

Fidel Castro and South African President Nelson Mandela.
CREDIT: ARCHIVAL

---

[43] Nelson Mandela, *Conversations with Myself*, p. 389

Castro fired his own son

Castro's eldest son, Fidelito, studied nuclear science in the Soviet Union. He was head of the Cuban Atomic Energy Commission from 1980-1992. Castro had Fidelito fired when he mishandled Cuba's nuclear program. "There was no resignation," Fidel said. "He was fired for incompetence. We don't have a monarchy here." [44]

There have been more than 600 assassination attempts to kill Fidel Castro

"If surviving assassination attempts were an Olympic event, then I would win the gold medal."— Fidel Castro

Fabian Escalante, the man who was once the head of the Cuban secret service, calculated that there had been a total of 638 attempts to kill Fidel Castro.

That was, at the time, an average of about 13.5 attempts a year since the Revolution. These attempts and plans ranged from exploding cigars (actually attempted), to exploding shellfish (Castro was a scuba diver), poison pills, bacterial poisons, and just plain old shooting, which the CIA hoped a successful Bay of Pigs invasion would lead to. The CIA also considered embarrassing Castro (slip him something in his food that would cause the hair in his beard to fall out.) [45]

A more recent attempt took place in 2000 in Panama, where 200 pounds of explosives were to be set to go off under the podium where Castro would be speaking. The plot was thwarted and the would-be assassins were caught, tried, sentenced, and jailed. In one of her last acts as Panamanian president, Miraya Moscoso pardoned the ringleader, Luis Posada, a long-time CIA asset and Cuban exile who was wanted for trial in Venezuela. Posada eventually hopped a boat and illegally entered the United States, where the government reluctantly—but only after Posada kept going public—took him into custody.

The US government refuses to honor its extradition treaty with Venezuela and continues to try to decide what to do with Posada. Posada, by the way, was considered to be responsible for the in-air destruction of a Cubana Air flight in 1976 that carried seventy-three people, including the entire Cuban Olympic fencing team to their deaths.

Recommended viewing—

Fidel Castro speaks English after UN visit—http://youtu.be/d_OQBEDgwOc

---

[44] Ann Louise Bardach, "*Without Fidel: A Death Foretold in Miami, Havana, and Washington*"New York: Scribner (2009), p. 36

[45] http://en.wikipedia.org/wiki/Operation_Mongoose

Fidel Castro—US Wrongdoing—http://youtu.be/TjbLa50UxUw

Fidel Castro Interview – with Barbara Walters
http://youtu.be/qbUgUJuI6Ak

Fidel Castro's Warning to the World "Israel/US Strike on Iran will bring about Nuclear World War 3"
http://youtu.be/9PcpsKGZsuo

Fidel – The Untold Story—http://youtu.be/OkNm7BWcOl0

Raúl Castro

Raúl Castro has been with Fidel since the very beginning

Raúl Castro (center) with Fidel Castro on his left and
Che Guevara on his right
CREDIT: ARCHIVAL

Raúl Castro, former head of the armed forces since the Revolution, was elected President of the Republic of Cuba in 2008.

Raúl Castro fought alongside his older (by five years) brother from the beginning when both were students, in the Sierra Maestra during the rebellion, and as minister of the Armed Forces from 1959 to 2008. From 2006 to 2008 Raúl was also acting president, filling in for Fidel, who was on medical leave. At that time, when speaking to a group of university students, Raúl said, "Fidel is irreplaceable, unless we all replace him together."[46]

---

[46] http://news.bbc.co.uk/2/hi/americas/6199369.stm

Raúl Castro, current President of the Republic of Cuba
CREDIT: ROOSEWELT PINHEIRO/ABR

Raúl has always been the man who got things done

Raúl became a socialist before Fidel did, and it was Raúl who initiated contact with the Soviet Union. It was also Raúl who was the chief administrator in the Castro government, and he is reported to have been the prime mover behind the mass executions following the successful revolution.

In mid-January 1959, only three weeks after taking power, Fidel told a large crowd in Havana that if he were assassinated "behind me come others more radical than me." To make it clear who he meant, he then announced that his brother Raúl would be second-in-command of their revolutionary movement and also his designated successor. [47]

During the 1990s, Raúl Castro shrank the Cuban military by 80 percent

During the Special Period, after financial aid and subsidies from the Soviet Union had disappeared, Raúl Castro as head of the armed forces downsized the military by 80 percent, saying, "Beans are more important than guns." [48]

---

[47] Brian Ladell, *After Fidel: Raúl Castro and the Future of Cuba's Revolution*, Palgrave Macmillan, 2007, p. 11.

[48] http://www.reuters.com/article/2007/07/24/us-cuba-castro-idUSN243122220070724

Armed forces were no longer sent to assist foreign countries, as they had been to countries such as Angola, and instead were used primarily to transport produce to market and to work in the sugar cane fields.

Raúl and his brother Fidel both married women connected with Cuba's largest corporations

Raúl's wife was Vilma Espín, who did a year of post-graduate studies in chemical engineering at Massachusetts Institute of Technology, and then with the rebels in the Sierra Maestra. She married Raúl in January 1959, and founded the Federation of Cuban Women in 1960, heading that organization her entire life. Espín was the daughter of a wealthy lawyer for the Bacardi rum company, which has been one of the Castro government's greatest enemies since the revolution. She died in 2007.

Fidel's first wife was Mirta Díaz Balart, daughter of a wealthy lawyer for the American-owned United Fruit Company, which was an instigator of a number of government coups in Central and South America. Allen Dulles, director of the Central Intelligence Agency, had been a member of the board of trustees of United Fruit Company. His brother, John Foster Dulles, was US Secretary of State under President Eisenhower, and Foster Dulles' law firm represented United Fruit.

Fidel and Mirta married in 1948 and divorced in 1955 while Fidel was in exile. The properties of both Bacardi Rum and United Fruit Company were expropriated after the revolution.

Raúl Castro would like to see more cooperation with the United States

In 2008, after being the interim president for a year and a half, Raúl Castro was named president. In an interview with American actor-journalist Sean Penn, he said:

> The American people are among our closest neighbors. We should respect each other. We have never held anything against the American people. Good relations would be mutually advantageous. Perhaps we cannot solve all of our problems, but we can solve a good many of them. [49]

In the same interview, Raúl stated that the Cuban military and the US military had been holding regular monthly meetings since 1995. The meetings take place either at Guantánamo Naval Base or in Cuban-held

---

[49]   Sean Penn interview with Raúl Castro in *The Nation*, December 15, 2008

territory (as opposed to American-held Cuban territory). Topics concern the Guantánamo base, and include joint emergency-preparedness exercises. [50]

Raúl stated again in Guantanamo on July 26, 2012, on the day celebrating the attack on the Moncada Barracks:

> The day they [the United States] are ready, the table is set, and this has been communicated through the regular diplomatic channels. If they want to hold a discussion we will do so, but on equal terms, because we are no-one's subjects, nor a colony, nor anyone's puppets...If they want confrontation, it must be in sports, preferably baseball, nothing else. [51]

Raúl Castro is now president of the Community of Latin American and Caribbean States (CELAC)

In January 2013, Castro was elected president pro tempore of CELAC, which is a cooperative bloc of 33 countries from Mexico to the southern tip of South America. It includes every country in the Americas—including, of course, Cuba—except for those few, small territories controlled by France, Denmark, the Netherlands, and the United Kingdom.

CELAC is intended to be an alternative to the Organization of American States (OAS), which was founded by, and has always been controlled by, the United States. In fact, CELAC specifically excludes the US and Canada.

Website—http://www.celac.gob.ve/

Recommended viewing—

Raúl calls for change at top of Cuba—http://youtu.be/WO3PNsl5Z_0

---

[50] Sean Penn in *The Nation*, December 15, 2008

[51] Prensa Latina http://bit.ly/WkHlzQ

Relations with the US

The US government has always considered the Caribbean its own "inland sea." This is readily apparent in the number of times the US has sent its military forces into various Caribbean countries as well as Central and South American countries bordering the Caribbean. Cuba, Haiti, Dominican Republic, Grenada, Mexico, Guatemala, Panama, Nicaragua, Colombia, Puerto Rico and Honduras all come to mind.

Cuba's uprising against Spanish control was nearing total success in 1898 when the Americans entered the war, declared themselves the winner, and took control not only of Cuba, but of an even more important goal, the Philippines.

The US government—and US corporations—controlled Cuba either directly or indirectly for more than half a century. The successful Cuban Revolution ended not only control by Fulgencio Batista, but by the United States as well.

The US government canceled its sugar contract with Cuba, attacked at the Bay of Pigs, is still continuing its embargo—which was made even more vindictive by the Torricelli and Helms-Burton Acts,—and attempted numerous assassination attempts on Fidel Castro. It has conducted operations to destroy Cuban crops, supported the bombing of a Cuban civilian airplane and the murder of all its passengers, used a "coaling station" on Cuban soil as a torture center, and has refused for more than 50 years to allow Americans their basic right to visit a neighboring country. The US government's executive branch, Congress, military, Central Intelligence Agency, and allied Cuban-American terrorists have made clear their contempt for Cuba, its people, and their right to self-determination. But, despite all of these efforts by the most powerful nation on earth, they have failed to destroy the country, the society and the will of the Cuban people.

US Attacks

US attempts to overthrow the Cuban government began a year after the successful revolution

On April 6, 1960, Lester D. Mallory, US Deputy Assistant Secretary of State for Inter-American Affairs, wrote an internal memorandum titled: "Inauguration by the US government of a policy to weaken the Cuban economy, April-July 1960." In the memorandum, Mallory stated,

> The majority of Cubans support Castro (the lowest estimate I have seen is 50 percent).
>
> There is no effective political opposition.
>
> Militant opposition to Castro from without Cuba would only serve his and the communist cause.
>
> The only foreseeable means of alienating internal support is through disenchantment and disaffection based on economic dissatisfaction and hardship.
>
> If the above are accepted or cannot be successfully countered, it follows that every possible means should be undertaken promptly to weaken the economic life of Cuba. If such a policy is adopted, it should be the result of a positive decision which would call forth a line of action which, while as adroit and inconspicuous as possible, makes the greatest inroads in denying money and supplies to Cuba, to decrease monetary and real wages, to bring about hunger, desperation and overthrow of government. [52]

Fifty years later the US government is still trying to create hunger and desperation in Cuba in order to overthrow its government.

Smedley Butler

Two-time Medal of Honor winner General Smedley Butler wrote: "I was a gangster for capitalism"

US Marine Corps General Smedley Butler, 1881-1940, was awarded the Congressional Medal of Honor twice, and was the most decorated Marine in US history at the time of his death.

---

[52] http://bit.ly/XTTUSL

General Smedley Butler.
CREDIT: US MARINE CORPS / WIKIMEDIA COMMONS

General Butler served in Cuba, among many other places. Here is what he had to say about his work there and his military career:

> I spent 33 years and four months in active military service and during that period I spent most of my time as a high class muscle man for Big Business, for Wall Street and the bankers. In short, I was a racketeer, a gangster for capitalism. I helped make Mexico and especially Tampico safe for American oil interests in 1914. I helped make Haiti and Cuba a decent place for the National City Bank boys to collect revenues in. I helped in the raping of half a dozen Central American republics for the benefit of Wall Street. I helped purify Nicaragua for the International Banking House of Brown Brothers in 1902–1912. I brought light to the Dominican Republic for the American sugar interests in 1916. I helped make Honduras right for the American fruit companies in 1903. In China in 1927 I helped see to it that Standard Oil went on its way unmolested.
>
> —from a speech in 1935

Butler had a similar point of view of war in general:

> War is just a racket. A racket is best described, I believe, as something that is not what it seems to the majority of people. Only a small inside group knows what it is about. It is conducted for the benefit of the very few at the expense of the masses.

81

> I believe in adequate defense at the coastline and nothing else. If
> a nation comes over here to fight, then we'll fight. The trouble
> with America is that when the dollar only earns 6 percent over
> here, then it gets restless and goes overseas to get 100 percent.
> Then the flag follows the dollar and the soldiers follow the flag.

> I wouldn't go to war again as I have done to protect some lousy
> investment of the bankers. There are only two things we should
> fight for. One is the defense of our homes and the other is the
> Bill of Rights. War for any other reason is simply a racket. [53]

Recommended viewing—

Universal Newsreel - Gen. Butler bares plot by fascists
http://youtu.be/uo1hp_LMGF8

Guantánamo Bay Naval Base

Cuba does not cash the rent checks from the US for Guantánamo Bay Naval Base

Every year the US government sends a rent check to the Cuban government.
The US no longer pays in gold, but the annual $2,000 payment has more than
doubled due to inflation.

The Cuban government has cashed only one of those checks since the
Revolution in 1959, and that cashing was an accident, according to Fidel
Castro. [54]

President Theodore Roosevelt signed the lease agreement in 1903, 56 years
before the current Cuban government began.

> The United States of America agrees and covenants to pay to
> the Republic of Cuba the annual sum of two thousand dollars,
> in gold coin of the United States, as long as the former shall
> occupy and use said areas of land by virtue of said agreement.

---

[53] www.informationclearinghouse.info/article4377.htm (includes 29 minute audio
documentary)

[54] www.reuters.com/article/2007/08/17/idUSN17200921 http://reut.rs/RAL6vb

—Signed at Habana, July 2, 1903
Approved by the President, October 2, 1903
Ratified by the President of Cuba, August 17, 1903

McDonald's restaurant at Guantánamo Naval Base, Cuba.
CREDIT: WIKIMEDIA COMMONS

The US government is in violation of its lease for Guantánamo Bay

The lease agreement limits use of the Cuban territory to "coaling and naval purposes only," neither of which appears to cover the prison or tribunal operations. The agreement also expressly prohibits "commercial, industrial or other enterprise within said areas," yet the base now sports a McDonald's, two Starbucks, a Subway sandwich shop and other US concessions.

The agreement was originally signed in 1903 and revised in 1934, both times with Cuban governments that were basically puppets of the US government. Cuba's government since 1959, which had no say about the agreement, has had no ability to change the lease agreement because the agreement says that any changes have to be agreed to by both Cuba and the United States, and the US government refuses to make any changes.

Life at Guantánamo can be very comfortable

Here is information on Guantánamo direct from the US naval base's official website: [55]

---

[55] US Navy   US Navy http://www.cnic.navy.mil/Guantanamo/index.htm

Naval Base Guantanamo Bay is a great community as well. Since we do not have the luxury of leaving the base after work, we have everything you need right here. We have a Commissary, Navy Exchange, furniture store, gas station, hospital, dry cleaners, bowling alley, library, Navy Federal Credit Union, Community Bank, and Columbia College so you can work on advancing your education. If you are accompanied by your family and have children, we have both an elementary (pre-K through 6th grade) and high school (grades 7-12), along with two Child Development Centers and a Youth Center. All facilities are open to the general population with the exception of the base clubs. The drinking age on base is 21, so only personnel 21 and older are allowed into the clubs.

Windjammer Pool, US Naval Station, Guantanamo Bay.
CREDIT: US NAVY

The base has a very diverse and rich culture. Our current population is about 8,500. In addition to active duty service members from the Navy, Army, Marine Corps, Air Force, Coast Guard, and their dependents, we have civilian contractors, DoD contractors, dependents of hired contractors and third country nationals (TCN), mostly from Jamaica and the Philippines. The base contractors hire many of the TCNs for their workforce. Because of this diverse population mixture, we commemorate each other's special celebrations such as Cuban-American Friendship Day, Philippine Independence Day, and Jamaican Independence Day.

Guantanamo Bay is not all work. There are many off-duty activities as well. Most activities are outdoors, because we have great weather. Because of our location, the temperature in the winter is in the 60s in the morning and is in the upper 70s by afternoon. During the summer the temperature is in the mid 70s in the morning, and rises into the upper 90s throughout the day. MWR [Morale, Welfare and Recreation] is very active here. We have free outdoor movie theaters that show first run movies every night, with two on the weekends. Intramural sports are very popular and are programmed throughout the year, and there are a number of different ball fields in various locations around the base. Additionally MWR has boats, kayaks, fishing equipment, diving equipment, and even some surfboards for rent. We have a 9-hole golf course, an 18-hole miniature golf course, tennis courts, batting cages, and three swimming pools. There is great diving here. You can snorkel or tank dive. If you are not a certified diver, you can take classes to become certified. Night dives are very popular with certified divers.

You can even have a 'GTMO Getaway Weekend.' We have a bachelor quarters complex on the Leeward side of the base which has 134 rooms. You can take the ferry over to the Leeward side and rent a room for about $7. Additionally there is a galley on Leeward side, an outdoor movie theater (coming soon), a mini-mart, and a small club. You can spend the weekend away from everyone, visit one of the Leeward side's four beaches and relax.

Not everyone at the Guantanamo Bay Naval Base enjoys the same comforts

Since 2002, the base has also included the Guantanamo Bay Detention Camp where 779 prisoners of the "War on Terrorism" have been held. Some prisoners have been as young as thirteen years of age; most have been determined to be guilty of no crimes, yet a number of these people considered innocent by the US government are still being held.

Camp Delta, US Naval Station, Guantanamo Bay, Cuba.
CREDIT: US NAVY

Cuba for the Misinformed

Prisoners at Camp Delta, US Naval Station, Guantanamo Bay, Cuba.
CREDIT: SHANE T. MCCOY, US NAVY

It is also a location where a number of prisoners have been subject to "enhanced interrogation;" torture techniques which are identical to those for which the US government executed Germans and Japanese as war criminals after World War II.

School of the Americas

The US military's school has trained assassins, torturers and dictators since 1946

The School of the Americas (SOA) was established by the US military in Panama in 1946 and originally named the Latin American Ground School.

The school's mission was "to provide professional education and training" while "promoting democratic values, respect for human rights, and knowledge and understanding of United States customs and traditions." Its students were initially members from both the US military and military forces throughout Latin America.

In 1946 the school was renamed the US Army Caribbean School–Spanish Instruction. Since 1956 it has focused on Latin American soldiers and officers, and all instruction has been in Spanish.

In 1963, several years after the Cuban Revolution, it was renamed the US Army School of the Americas. Its curriculum was changed from "nation building"—bridge-building, well-digging, food preparation, and equipment maintenance and repair, to "counterinsurgency"—combating growing "communist inspired,"(populist) movements throughout Latin America.

Following the signing of the Panama Canal Treaty, the school moved in 1984 to Fort Benning, Georgia. As a result of negative publicity resulting from the media and from Congressional hearings, in 2000 the school was renamed the Western Hemisphere Institute for Security Cooperation.

The Congressional hearings had resulted from charges that the US Army was running a "torture school" that violated civil rights. In 1996, the Pentagon released seven training manuals used at the school between 1987 and 1991. According to the Pentagon's own summary of the manuals, they covered such techniques for acquiring information from suspects as "beatings, false imprisonment, executions and the use of truth serums."

Since 2004, all students are required to receive eight hours of instruction in "human rights, the rule of law, due process, civilian control of the military, and the role of the military in a democratic society." When one looks at the human rights violations conducted by the following list of graduates, one might question whether a total of only eight hours on such topics is sufficient.

Graduates of the US School of the Americas include notables from the following countries:

Panama

Manual Noriega, dictator/leader of Panama and a former agent of the CIA's George H. W. Bush and CIA employees during Noriega's 30-year employment. Noriega became president of Panama in a coup. US President George H.W. Bush invaded Panama to capture Noriega on "drug charges." The invasion resulted in as many as 3,000 civilian deaths.

Argentina

General Leopoldo Galtierri, former head of the Argentine military junta, was implicated in the kidnapping, disappearance and deaths of as many as 30,000 Argentine civilians during the "Dirty War" (1976-1983).

El Salvador

Roberto d'Aubuisson, head of a unit of death squads in El Salvador and the assassin of Archbishop Oscar Romero. D'Aubuisson was also connected with the 1989 massacre in El Mozote, El Salvador, in which 900 men, women and children were murdered.

Also in El Salvador, nineteen of the twenty-seven men involved in the murder of six Jesuit priests, their housekeeper and her teenage daughter at the University of Central America.

Haiti

General Raoul Cedras, who overthrew the democratically elected government of Jean-Bertrand Aristide in Haiti in 1991. During his term of running the country until 1994, he was responsible for the death of more than 5,000 people.

Peru

General Hugo Banzer Suarez who became dictator of Peru in 1971 after a coup. Among his accomplishments were sheltering Klaus Barbie, the Nazi war criminal known as the "Butcher of Lyon."

Chile

Manuel Contreras, head of Chile's secret police during the Pinochet dictatorship.

Other

Other graduates terrorized their countrymen in Bolivia, Honduras, Guatemala, Ecuador, Peru and Chile (where one out of every seven members of the notorious DINA—the intelligence agency responsible for many of the worst atrocities during Pinochet's reign—was an SOA graduate).

Recommended viewing—

School of the Americas, School of Assassins—http://youtu.be/HOeaG6-qsVc

Nationalization of Companies

The United States has refused to accept compensation for nationalized corporations in Cuba

After the Cuban Revolution, the new Cuban government offered to negotiate settlements with all foreign corporations whose companies and properties in Cuba had been taken over by the revolutionary government.

Only the US government refused to negotiate with Cuba. *All* other countries—including Canada, France, Italy, Mexico, Spain, Switzerland, and the United Kingdom—reached settlements, and their companies were all compensated by the Cuban government.

The Cuban government could have ignored the claims, just as the government under US President George Washington did when payment was demanded by dispossessed Tories and Loyalists after the Revolutionary War. The United States could have negotiated a settlement with Cuba, just as the

Americans had done with Mexico after the Mexican oil expropriations in 1938. Instead, the US government has refused any negotiations.

Bay of Pigs

The Bay of Pigs has nothing to do with pigs

In Spanish, *cochino* means *pig*. But not with the Bay of Pigs, which in Spanish is *Bahía de Cochinos*. "Cochinos" is a common name for a type of triggerfish that lives in coral reefs in the bay.

Cubans know the Bay of Pigs as *Playa Girón*

In 1961, approximately 1500 anti-government Cubans, trained and supported by the US Central Intelligence Agency, invaded Cuba at a location referred to by Americans as the *Bay of Pigs* and by Cubans as Playa Girón, *Girón* (named after a French pirate in the early 1600s) being the name of a beach on the bay where the invasion actually took place. The goal was to bring about the overthrow of the Castro government.

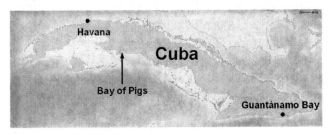

Location of Bay of Pigs invasion
CREDIT: ZLEITZEN/WIKIPEDIA COMMONS

The Cuban exiles who took part in the invasion named themselves *Brigade 2506*. Each member of the group had a number—starting with 2500 in order to make the force look larger than it actually was. Brigade member 2506 (Carlos Rafael Santana Estevez) was killed in a training accident, and the brigade was named in his honor.

The invasion force landed on Cuba's Caribbean coast 125 miles south of Havana. Although 176 Cubans were killed and more than 300 wounded, the attacking force was defeated. 114 of them were killed and more than 1,000 taken prisoner. Cuba released them in 1962 in exchange for $53 million in food and medicine from the United States.

Brigade 2506 prisoners captured by Cuban troops at the Bay of Pigs invasion.
CREDIT: MIGUEL VINAS/AFP

Che Guevara thanked President Kennedy for the Bay of Pigs Invasion

On August 17, 1961, four months after the Bay of Pigs invasion, US President John F. Kennedy's aide Richard Goodwin met secretly with Che Guevara in Argentina. Goodwin afterwards reported the following to President Kennedy:

> He [Che Guevara] then went on to say that he wanted to thank us very much for the invasion—that it had been a great political victory for them—enabled them to consolidate—and transformed them from an aggrieved little country into an equal. [56]

Cubans were still learning how to operate their Russian-made tanks when they were invaded at the Bay of Pigs

In 2008 actor-activist Sean Penn interviewed Cuban president Raúl Castro who told him, "You know, Sean, there was a famous picture of Fidel from the Bay of Pigs invasion. He is standing in front of a Russian tank. We did not yet know even how to put those tanks in reverse. So," he jokes, "retreat was no option!" [57]

---

[56] www.gwu.edu/~nsarchiv/bayofpigs/19610822.pdf

[57] Sean Penn, "Conversations with Chavez and Castro," *The Nation,* Dec. 15, 2008.

Fidel Castro in Russian-supplied tank at the
Bay of Pigs.
CREDIT: ARCHIVAL

Recommended Viewing—

Cuba Invaded—http://archive.org/details/1961-04-19_Cuba_Invaded

Secrets of the CIA – Bay of Pigs—http://youtu.be/DoGESE_wO34

John F. Kennedy speech on the Bay of Pigs (audio)
www.jfklibrary.org/Asset-Viewer/Archives/JFKWHA-024-001.aspx

Che Guevara speech on the Bay of Pigs—http://youtu.be/ggioi2Ixb9U

Bay of Pigs Invasion
Khan Academy—http://bit.ly/WjMW9x

Operation Mongoose

President Kennedy initiated sabotage and assassination in Cuba

Operation Mongoose, also known as the "Cuban Project," was the overall name for CIA operations initiated by President John F. Kennedy on November 30, 1961. Kennedy authorized these covert operations against the Cuban government after the failure of the US-backed Bay of Pigs invasion. The goal was an "open revolt and overthrow of the Communist regime" by October 1962.

The more than thirty plans and operations included propaganda activities, sabotage, assassination of government officials—particularly Fidel Castro—placing US Special Forces guerrillas in Cuba, destroying sugar crops, and mining Cuban harbors. [58]

Operation Northwoods

The US military wanted to attack targets in the United States, including civilians, and blame it on Cuba

In 1962, US Army General Lyman Lemnitzer, the Chairman of the US Joint Chiefs of Staff, which is composed of the heads of all US military services, presented to then-Secretary of Defense Robert McNamara a plan called Operation Northwoods, part of the guiding philosophy of Operation Mongoose. The purpose was to conduct a terror campaign *in the United States* which would justify—to the American public—intervention in Cuba.

The full Operation Northwoods document is at:
http://www.smeggys.co.uk/operation_northwoods.php

---

[58] https://en.wikipedia.org/wiki/Operation_Mongoose

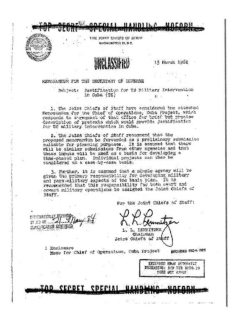

Cover page for Operation Northwoods.
CREDIT: US GOVERNMENT/ NATIONAL SECURITY ARCHIVE AT
THE GEORGE WASHINGTON UNIVERSITY

Components of the plan included real and simulated attacks which would be blamed on the Cuban government ("false flag" operations.) Many of these attacks would take place in the United States against Cuban exiles, US military targets, and American civilians.

Proposals included staging mock attacks, sabotage and riots at Guantánamo Bay Naval Base and blaming it on Cuban forces; firebombing and sinking an American ship at the Guantánamo Bay base (first choice: using a manned ship with real US Navy casualties; second choice: unmanned ship with fake funerals); destroying American aircraft and blaming it on the Cubans; *destroying an unmanned drone masquerading as a commercial aircraft supposedly full of "college students off on a holiday,"* [author's emphasis] and the "real or simulated" sinking of boatloads of Cuban refugees. [59] Proposals in Operation Northwoods also included a terror campaign in Miami and perhaps even Washington, D.C. The proposals were approved by the Joint Chiefs of Staff but turned down by the Kennedy administration.

---

[59] http://en.wikipedia.org/wiki/Operation_Northwoods

Cuba for the Misinformed

The following excerpt from pages 7 and 8 is an example of the Operation Northwoods document approved by the US Joint Chiefs of Staff. [60]

> A series of well coordinated incidents will be planned to take place in and around Guantánamo to give genuine appearance of being done by hostile Cuban forces.
>
> Incidents to establish a credible attack:
>
> 1. Start rumors (many). Use clandestine radio.
>
> 2. Land friendly Cubans in uniform "over-the-fence" to stage attack on base.
>
> 3. Capture Cuban (friendly) saboteurs inside the base.
>
> 4. Start riots near the base main gate (friendly Cubans).
>
> 5. Blow up ammunition inside the base: start fires.
>
> 6. Burn aircraft on air base (sabotage).
>
> 7. Lob mortar shells from outside of base into base.
>
> 8. Capture assault teams approaching from the sea or vicinity of Guantánamo City.
>
> 9. Capture militia group which storms base.
>
> 10. Sabotage ship in harbor; large fires – naphthalene.
>
> 11. Sink ship near harbor entrance. Conduct funerals for mock-victims.
>
> 12. A "Remember the Maine" incident could be arranged: We could blow up a US ship in Guantánamo Bay and blame Cuba. Casualty lists in US newspapers would cause a helpful wave of national indignation.
>
> 13. We could develop a Communist Cuban terror campaign in the Miami area, in other Florida cities and even in Washington.

And here is more from page 10 of the Operation Northwoods proposal. Note that this was written in 1962, thirty-nine years before the 9/11 attack on the World Trade Center in New York City.

> 8. It is possible to create an incident which will demonstrate convincingly that a Cuban aircraft has attacked and shot down a chartered civil airliner en route from the United States to Jamaica, Guatemala, Panama or Venezuela. The destination

---

[60] http://en.wikipedia.org/wiki/Operation_Northwoods

would be chosen only to cause the flight plan to cross Cuba. The passengers could be a group of college students off on a holiday or any grouping of persons with a common interest to support chartering a non-scheduled flight.

a. An aircraft at Eglin AFB would be painted and numbered as an exact duplicate for a civil registered aircraft belonging to a CIA proprietary organization in the Miami area. At the designated time the duplicate would be substituted for the actual civil aircraft and would be loaded with selected passengers, all boarded under carefully prepared aliases. The actual aircraft would be converted to a drone.

b. Take off time of the drone aircraft and the actual aircraft will be scheduled to allow a rendezvous south of Florida. From the rendezvous point the passenger-carrying aircraft will descend to minimum altitude and go directly into an auxiliary field at Eglin AFB where arrangements will have been made to evacuate the passengers and return the aircraft to its original status. The drone aircraft meanwhile will continue to fly the filed flight plan. When over Cuba the drone will be transmitting on the international distress frequency a "MAY DAY" message stating he is under attack by Cuban MIG aircraft. The transmission will be interrupted by destruction of the aircraft which will be triggered by radio signal. [61]

The full Operation Northwoods document can be seen at the website in the footnote below. [62]

Cuban Missile Crisis

The United States gave in as much as the Soviet Union to end the missile crisis

In October 1962, the United States confronted the Soviet Union over the USSR's placement of nuclear-armed missiles in Cuba. At the time there were 43,000 Soviet troops [63] and forty-two medium-range and intermediate-range ballistic missiles on the island.

On October 28, Soviet Premier Nikita Khrushchev sent a message to US President John F. Kennedy confirming the agreement that the Soviet Union would remove its missiles in return for the US agreeing to not again attack Cuba (as it had already done at the Bay of Pigs in 1961.) In a secret

---

[61] http://www2.gwu.edu/~nsarchiv/coldwar/documents/episode-10/02-06.htm

[62] http://www.smeggys.co.uk/operation_northwoods.php

[63]   http://www.nytimes.com/1992/01/15/world/us-underestimated-soviet-force-in-cuba-during-62-missile-crisis.html

agreement, the US government also agreed to remove its own nuclear missiles in Turkey which had directly threatened the USSR.

Fidel Castro wanted the Soviet Union to attack the US with nuclear weapons if the Americans invaded Cuba

On October 26, 1962 Castro believed the US would attack Cuba within the next 24-72 hours. He expected an attack either by air or a land invasion. He wrote to Soviet Premier Nikita Khrushchev:

> If the second variant [invasion] takes place and the imperialists invade Cuba with the aim of occupying it, the dangers of their aggressive policy are so great that after such an invasion the Soviet Union must never allow circumstances in which the imperialists could carry out a nuclear first strike against it.
>
> I tell you this because I believe that the imperialists' aggressiveness makes them extremely dangerous, and that if they manage to carry out an invasion of Cuba--a brutal act in violation of universal and moral law--then that would be the moment to eliminate this danger forever, in an act of the most legitimate self-defense. However harsh and terrible the solution, there would be no other. [64]

Not everyone was pleased with the peaceful resolution of the Cuban Missile Crisis

Some members of the US Joint Chiefs of Staff were very angry, particularly since the Cubans had shot down an American U2 aircraft that had (illegally) flown over Cuba.

Lockheed U-2 reconnaissance aircraft
CREDIT: US AIR FORCE

---

[64] Letter to Nikita Khrushchev from Fidel Castro regarding defending Cuban air space— http://www.cubanet.org/ref/dis/10110201.htm

Admiral George Anderson reportedly complained "we have been had," while Air Force General Curtis LeMay said the US should "go in and make a strike on Monday anyway." LeMay had previously urged an attack on targets in Cuba with air strikes and a ground invasion, saying that thanks to its powerful Strategic Air Command, the US now had the "Russian bear" "by the balls." "Now that we have gotten him in a trap, let's take his leg off right up to his testicles. On second thought, let's take his testicles off, too." [65]

The American military's unhappiness with the Kennedy-Khrushchev agreement was shared by Fidel Castro, who had not been consulted or informed of the decision to remove the missiles beforehand. He reportedly went into a rage, cursing Khrushchev as a "son of a bitch, bastard, asshole." A few days later, in a public speech at the University of Havana, Castro said that Khrushchev lacked *cojones* (balls).

After hearing that the Soviets had agreed to remove their missiles, Castro had even gone to a Cuban air force base in order to shoot down a US low-altitude aircraft himself, but none passed over the base. [66]

Recommended viewing—

Cuban Missile Crisis Documentary—http://youtu.be/KA4eGeVjy8Q

Defcon 2 – Cuban Missile Crisis—http://youtu.be/Jwz7YAQj-r0

Cuban Missile Crisis – Khan Academy—http://bit.ly/PNMQVg

Fidel Castro almost had control of 100 nuclear missiles of his own

In 2012 it was revealed that, although the Soviets had promised to remove all of their long-range nuclear missiles, there were still other missiles on the island. The Soviets agreed to remove those missiles specified by the Americans. However, American intelligence had not discovered 100 *tactical* nuclear missiles that the Soviets had also installed on the island.

---

[65] Michael Dobbs, *One Minute to Midnight: Kennedy, Khrushchev, and Castro on the Brink of Nuclear War*, Vintage (2009), p. 22.

[66] National Security Archives, p. 380   http://bit.ly/U0rH5j

Cuba for the Misinformed

Soviet ambassador Anastas Mikoyan (right)
with Fidel Castro and Che Guevara
CREDIT: ARCHIVAL

USSR President Nikita Khrushchev considered leaving those missiles in the hands of the Cubans in order to calm down Fidel Castro's outrage over the major missile pullout. Khrushchev dispatched Anastas Mikoyan to Cuba to meet with Castro. However, after a few days Mikoyan determined that Castro was too emotionally unstable about the Americans to be given control of the missiles, particularly as Castro had ordered his forces to shoot down any US planes that flew over the island. Mikoyan informed Castro that although the Soviet government wanted to leave the missiles with the Cubans, there was an unpublished Soviet law (actually, it did not exist) prohibiting them from transferring the missiles to another country's control. Castro finally accepted the situation, and the Soviets removed those missiles as well.[67] [68] [69]

---

[67] http://www.bbc.co.uk/news/magazine-19930260

[68] Foreign Policy http://bit.ly/RysIEJ

[69] Mikoyan memorandum—http://bit.ly/RE8qX2

Cubana Airlines Flight 455

Cuban exiles living in Florida murdered 78 people and were never charged by the United States

In 1976 two time bombs exploded on Cubana Airlines Flight 455 on its way from Barbados to Jamaica. Among the dead were all 24 members of the 1975 Cuban national fencing team.

Cubana McDonnell Douglas DC-8-43 CU-T1201, MAY 1976 at Madrid (MAD), © Pedro de la Cruz

Cubana Flight 455
CREDIT: PEDRO DE LA CRUZ

Evidence implicated anti-Castro Cuban exiles in Florida, all linked to the CIA, including Luis Posada Carriles. In 1998 Posada [70] had admitted to the New York Times [71] that he had masterminded the bombing of a Cuban hotel in 1997 that killed an Italian tourist.

---

[70] Spanish-speaking countries often use two surnames. In this case Posada is the patronym (father's last name) and Carrilles the matronym (mother's last name), but are generally referred to by the patronym (Luis Posada.)

[71] New York Times http://nyti.ms/SI0Hvt

70, LT. LUIS C. POSADA CARRILES
Oficial Inteligencia Escalon Retgdia.
Brigada 2506

Luis Posada - *Brigade 2506* member and terrorist.
CREDIT: US GOVERNMENT /
WIKIMEDIA COMMONS

Posada was convicted in Panama of involvement in the aircraft bombing, as well as in an assassination attempt on Fidel Castro in Panama in 2000 that, if carried out, would have killed hundreds of innocent people, primarily students at the University of Panama. In 2004 Posada was pardoned by Panamanian President Mireya Moscoso in the last days of her term, just before she moved to Miami, home of the largest Cuban exile community in the United States.

In 2008, the Supreme Court of Panama declared Moscoso's pardon unconstitutional, and in January 2012 the courts confirmed the sentencing of Posada and others. The US government has ignored its extradition treaty with Panama and Posada now lives in Miami.

Some of the victims of Cubana 455 terrorist attack.
CREDIT: BILL WEAVER/NARCOSPHERE

Recommended viewing—

Cubana Flight 455—http://youtu.be/uspkEV_fFzs

United States Interests Section

The US Government has a large official building complex in the country it doesn't officially recognize

Since the US government does not officially recognize the government which has been running Cuba since 1959, it does not have an ambassador or embassy in Cuba. It does, however, have an "interests section" headed by a "Chief of Mission." The Interests Section is formally attached to the Swiss Embassy—which is actually eight kilometers away—so its official title is the United States Interests Section of the Embassy of Switzerland. The Cuban Interests Section in Washington, D.C. has the same arrangement.

Cuba for the Misinformed

US Interests Section, Havana, Cuba.
CREDIT: KROKODYL / WIKIMEDIA COMMONS

The stated functions of the US Interests Section are:

> ...similar to those of any US government presence abroad: Consular Services, a Political and Economic Section, a Public Diplomacy Program, and Refugee Processing unique to Cuba.

> "The objectives of USINT in Cuba are to promote a peaceful transition to a democratic system based on respect for rule of law, individual human rights and open economic and communication systems.

"Señor Imperialists: We have absolutely no fear of you" –
Billboard formerly across the street from the US Interests Section.

The Jose Martí Anti-Imperialist Tribune was a result of the Elián González affair

This outdoor stage is located in Havana in the *Plaza de la Dignidad* (Dignity Plaza) across the street from the US Interests Section. (This had formerly been the 4th of July Park honoring American Independence Day.) It opened in April 2000 after being rapidly constructed in connection with the "battle" over Elián González.

González, at the time six years old, had been taken from Havana by his mother—without knowledge of his father—when she tried, along with others, to sail to Florida on a small boat. The boat capsized, the mother and ten others died, but Elián and two others survived and were taken to Florida.

A legal struggle ensued between his father's relatives in Florida who wanted Elián to stay in the United States and his father who wanted him returned to Cuba. US courts finally ruled in the father's favor and Elián went back to Cuba.

Each black flag with a white star represents a Cuban victim of terrorism, including the 78 people killed on Cubana Flight 455
CREDIT: MARSHALL SOULES

At other times the Cuban flag is flown
CREDIT: MARSHALL SOULES

Elián González (smiling) re-united with his father.
CREDIT: US GOVERNMENT

Statue of Jose Martí holding his son
(representing Elián González) and pointing
toward US Interests Section), Havana.

Beyond the legal battle, a propaganda battle was waged between the US government and the Cuban government. The Cuban government built the Anti-Imperialist Platform as a location for demonstrations, then and in the future, against the US government, as well as for other rallies and events.

On two of the platform's steel towers are concrete bases on which brass plaques have been mounted. One set of plaques bear the names of Cuban and other Latin American patriots—including Simon Bolivar, Salvador Allende, Augusto Cesar Sandino, Benito Juarez, Omar Torrijos, Ernesto Che Guevara, Charles M. de Céspedes, Antonio Maceo, and Maximo Gomez. Another pedestal honors Karl Marx, Frederick Engels and Vladimir Illich Lenin.

Still other plaques bear the names of US citizens honored in Cuba including Martin Luther King, Jr., Malcolm X, the martyrs of Haymarket Square, Henry Reeve, Clara Burton, Ralph Waldo Emerson, Mark Twain, Waldo Frank, Ernest Hemingway, Henry Wadsworth Longfellow, Helen Keller, Jane Addams, Nat Turner, Abraham Lincoln, Thomas Edison, Linus Pauling, Frank Lloyd Wright, Frederick Douglas, Dr. Benjamin Spock, Walt Whitman, Herbert Matthews, John Reed, and Phillip Foner.

The 138 flags at the plaza were added in 2006. Each flag has a white star against a black background and they represent Cuban victims of terrorism, including the 78 people killed on Cubana Flight 455 in 1976. The flags also served the purpose of blocking the view of the scrolling electronic billboard that the US Interests Section had placed on the outside of its fifth floor to deliver messages critical of the Cuban government. The flags were installed in February, one month after the billboard was installed. In June 2009 the US government removed the billboard, acknowledging that it had not been effective, particularly because Cubans could not see the messages because of the flags. [72]

Torricelli Act

The United States has blockaded Cuba just as the USSR did to West Berlin

The Torricelli Act is a US Congressional Act signed by President George H.W. Bush in 1992 and put into force by President Bill Clinton. The Torricelli Act made the embargo of Cuba even more severe by preventing food and medicine from being shipped to Cuba. The only exemption was for humanitarian aid. Before this act, 75 percent of the US trade with Cuba *had been* food and medicine so the new measure had serious effects on the Cuban people.

The original embargo of Cuba had intentionally *not* prevented shipment of food and medicine because that was exactly what the USSR had done when it blockaded West Berlin in 1948-1949. The Americans did not want to look like they were treating Cuba the same way that the USSR had treated Berlin. However, once the Soviet Union collapsed, the Americans felt safe to enforce the same measures against Cuba.

---

[72] CNN   http://bit.ly/So6vXD

Unfortunately, the Cubans had no equivalent to the US Air Force to come to their rescue with food and medicine the way the Berliners had experienced. Cuba's previous ally, the Soviet Union, had collapsed, and men, women and children in Cuba had to experience extreme deprivation (see Special Period, p. 205).

Helms-Burton Act

The Helms-Burton Act has been condemned by countries all over the world

Furthering the effects of the Torricelli Act, this Congressional action in 1996 stated that international companies who traded with Cuba could not trade with the United States. It also prohibited foreign companies from "trafficking in" (using, buying or selling) property in Cuba that had formerly been owned by Cubans now exiled in the United States. Those Cubans who fled Cuba after the takeover had their property nationalized. (Cuba's government offered to pay compensation for this property and every country except the United States settled. The US government refused to even negotiate.)

The new law meant that international companies would have to choose between trading with Cuba (population 11 million) or the United States (population more than 300 million).

The act was condemned by countries throughout the world including Argentina, Brazil, Mexico, Canada, the UK and the European Union, for interfering with international law and national sovereignty. The EU declared that the act did not apply within EU countries; and UK law not only condemned it but established criminal sanctions for those who followed certain provisions of the American law. The Mexican government passed a law fining anyone who obeyed the act, and Canada passed a law countering the effects of the act.

Two members of the Canadian Parliament satirized Helms-Burton by proposing a bill—*The Godfrey-Milliken Bill*—that would penalize the US government for its nationalization of Tory property after the American Revolution. [73]

---

[73] Godfrey-Milliken Bill   http://bit.ly/VJVfWo

Cuban Five

The Cuban Five were imprisoned for spying against US-based terrorists, not against the United States itself

The Cuban Five, also known as the Miami Five, are five members of the Cuban Secret Service who were imprisoned in the United States for conspiracy to commit espionage.

Free the Cuban Five billboard.
CREDIT: INTERNATIONAL COMMITTEE FOR THE FREEDOM OF THE CUBAN 5

However, their target was *not* the United States and its national security secrets. The five intelligence officers were focused on Cuban expatriates in Florida who had been involved in terrorism against Cuba. They were protecting Cuba by attempting to get information about planned terrorist actions against Cuba by anti-Castro militantsThe Five did indeed collect important information. The Cuban government then contacted the US government and gave it that information, assuming that the Americans would take action against those planning terrorism within the United States, as such actions would be in violation of US law. Instead, the Americans arrested and imprisoned the five Cubans. The terrorists remained at large; the people providing the US government information about the terrorists went to prison.

As of publication of this book, one of the Cuban Five—Rene González—completed his 13-year term in October 2011 and is out of prison on probation for three years. He is not allowed to return to Cuba, although the US government did allow him a brief visit to see his dying brother. Requiring González to remain in the United States during his probation period simply continues his punishment. He is not allowed visits by his wife, and his personal safety is jeopardized due to the strong anti-Cuban government feelings of many in South Florida.

The other four—Gerardo Hernández, Antonio Guerrero, Ramón Labañino, and Fernando González —continue to serve their terms, each in a different prison.

Cuba for the Misinformed

Amnesty International has criticized the US government's treatment of the Cuban Five as "unnecessarily punitive and contrary both to standards for the humane treatment of prisoners and to states' obligation to protect family life" because the wives of René Gonzáles and Gerardo Hernández have not been allowed visas to visit their imprisoned husbands. [74]

Despite the protests of their defense attorneys to move the trial elsewhere, the Cuban Five were tried in a federal court in Miami, the center of the Cuban-exile and anti-Cuban government activity.

> Holding a trial for five Cuban intelligence agents in Miami is about as fair as a trial for an Israeli intelligence agent in Tehran. You'd need a lot more than a good lawyer to be taken seriously.
>
> — Robert Pastor, President Jimmy Carter's national security adviser for Latin America [75]

Communist Countries

The CIA does not officially consider Cuba to be a dictatorship

Despite the US government's rhetoric, the CIA does not officially describe Cuba as a "one-man dictatorship" or any kind of "dictatorship."

Here is how the CIA World Factbook describes the following countries: [76]

> China – "Communist state"
> Cuba – "Communist state"
> Laos – "Communist state"
> Vietnam – "Communist state"
> North Korea – "Communist state one-man dictatorship"

Note also that the US government currently allows American citizens to freely travel to China, Laos, and Vietnam—and even North Korea (with cautions)—although it considers all of them to be communist states. It does not allow travel to Cuba. The US government has diplomatic relations with China, Laos and Vietnam. It does not with Cuba. The US government allows wide open trade with China (to the tune of a current $1 trillion US trade deficit), Laos and Vietnam. It does not with Cuba. The US government allows

---

[74] www.amnesty.org/en/library/info/AMR51/093/2010

[75] http://archive.truthout.org/case-cuban-five-brings-up-nuanced-meaning-terrorism63207

[76] https://www.cia.gov/library/publications/the-world-factbook/index.html

American corporations to establish offices, factories and sales outlets in China, Laos and Vietnam. It does not with Cuba.

Immigrants

Illegal immigrants from Cuba are accepted in the United States if their feet touch dry land

Under current US policy, if a Cuban leaves Cuba (most frequently escapes are by boat) and reaches the United States, he or she is admitted to the country if their feet touch dry land. If, however, they are intercepted by the US Coast Guard—even just a few feet from shore—they are turned back and expatriated to Cuba.

This is the so-called "wet feet, dry feet" policy. (The title is inspired by the Dr. Seuss children's book *Wet Foot, Dry Foot, Low Foot, High Foot: Learn About Opposites,* which gives an indication of the maturity of the policy.) Such an enticing opportunity is offered to the citizens of no other country in the world, most obviously excluding refugees from an island right next to Cuba—Haiti.

An absurd instance of this policy took place in 2006 when the US Coast Guard found 15 Cubans, including four women and two children, who had climbed onto an old bridge piling in the Florida Keys. As over the years the piling had been cut off from the land, the Coast Guard determined that since the Cubans could not walk to land, their feet were "wet," and so deported the people to Cuba. Later in the year, some of that group tried again and were able to reach land close to the same location.

Note: If Cubans sail from Cuba to Mexico, make their way through Mexico and then come across into the United States at the Texas-Mexico border, they are also admitted and are referred to as "dusty foot" arrivals. [77]

Terrorism

The US government wrongly and cynically accuses Cuba of supporting terrorists

The US Department of State says that Cuba is a "totalitarian communist state." The CIA, not known to be soft on communism, calls it only a "communist state" (without the "totalitarian,") and further says that the "current government assumed power by force on January 1, 1959."

---

[77] Houston Press http://bit.ly/So63IZ

Cuba for the Misinformed

There is no mention, of course, that the US government had aided that "force" by cutting off all shipments of arms to Fulgencio Batista's forces on March 13, 1958—a blockade that kept weapons from the Batista government that the "force" overthrew. This happened after the US government had provided Batista with arms and money for years, until it realized he was going to lose to the revolutionary movement.

Cuba was first designated by the US State Department as a country that has "repeatedly provided support for acts of international terrorism" in 1982, due to its support for communist rebels in Africa and Latin America in the 1960s and 1970s.

Even so, the State Department Country Report on Terrorism in 2008 stated that Cuba "no longer actively supports armed struggles in Latin America and other parts of the world" and "The United States has no evidence of terrorist-related money laundering or terrorist financing activities in Cuba." [78]

A year later, the 2009 report stated, "There was no evidence of direct financial support for terrorist organizations by Cuba in 2009" and the 2010 report stated, "The Cuban government and official media publicly condemned acts of terrorism by al-Qa'ida and affiliates."

In its 2010 *Country Reports on Terrorism* the US State Department reports that Cuba is on the US list of state supporters of terrorism (along with Iran, Sudan and Syria) because:

> Designated as a State Sponsor of Terrorism in 1982, the Government of Cuba maintained a public stance against terrorism and terrorist financing in 2010, but there was no evidence that it had severed ties with elements from the Revolutionary Armed Forces of Colombia (FARC) and recent media reports indicate some current and former members of the Basque Fatherland and Liberty (ETA) continue to reside in Cuba. Available information suggested that the Cuban government maintained limited contact with FARC members, but there was no evidence of direct financial or ongoing material support. In March, the Cuban government allowed Spanish Police to travel to Cuba to confirm the presence of suspected ETA members. [79]

Here is what former US President Jimmy Carter reported about State Department charges concerning Cuba's allowing of members of FARC and ETA to live in Cuba after Carter met with a number of foreign ambassadors on his trip to Havana on March 28-30, 2011.

---

[78] Progreso Weekly   http://bit.ly/U0vRKv

[79] www.state.gov/j/ct/rls/crt/2010/170260.htm

> We raised a question about the terrorist list, and the Ambassadors from Spain and Colombia said they were not concerned about the presence of members of FARC, ETA, and ELN in Cuba. Indeed, they maintained that this enhances their ability to deal more effectively with these groups. In fact, ETA members are there at the request of the Spanish government. [80]

The State Department's *Country Reports on Terrorism 2010* also complains that:

> Cuba continued to denounce US counter-terrorism efforts throughout the world, portraying them as a pretext to extend US influence and power.

The third charge by the State Department is that:

> Cuba has been used as a transit point by third-country nationals looking to enter illegally into the United State.

In the very next sentence, the State Department negates this charge against Cuba by saying:

> The Government of Cuba is aware of the border integrity and transnational security concerns posed by such transit and investigated third country migrant smuggling and related criminal activities. In November, the government allowed representatives of the Transportation Security Administration to conduct a series of airport security visits throughout the island.[81]

So the State Department admits that Cuba has "investigated third country migrant smuggling" and has even allowed TSA representatives to visit airports throughout Cuba.

Shortly before publication of this book (December 2012), Cuba was hosting peace talks between the Colombian government and the Revolutionary Armed Forces of Colombia—People's Army. It would seem that Cuba could more properly be labeled a State Sponsor of Cooperation.

---

[80] www.cartercenter.org/news/trip_reports/cuba-march2011.html

[81] www.state.gov/j/ct/rls/crt/2010/170260.htm

Quotes

US government policy can be demonstrated not only by the actions of that country but by the statements of many of its leaders.

I candidly confess that I have ever looked on Cuba as the most interesting addition which could ever be made to our system of States. The control which, with Florida, this island would give us over the Gulf of Mexico, and the countries and isthmus bordering on it, as well as all those whose waters flow into it, would fill up the measure of our political well-being.

—*Former president Thomas Jefferson in a letter to US President James Monroe, Oct. 24, 1823.*

It is next to impossible to make them believe that we have only their own interests at heart.

—*Governor of Cuba US General Leonard Wood to Theodore Roosevelt (1901)*

Just at the moment I am so angry with that infernal little Cuban republic that I would like to wipe its people off the face of the earth. All that we wanted from them was that they would behave themselves and be prosperous and happy so that we would not have to interfere. [82]

—*President Theodore Roosevelt. a few years after his actions in Cuba*

I am doing my best to persuade the Cubans that if only they will be good they will be happy; I am seeking the very minimum of interference necessary to make them good.

—*President Theodore Roosevelt, when asked why he had sent in the Marines to take over Cuba in 1906*

We are here only to help you on. With our arm under your arm, lifting you again on the path of wonderful progress.

—*Secretary of War William Howard Taft to Cubans (1906)*

---

[82] Sept. 13, 1906, Roosevelt Papers, Library of Congress

[The end of the Cuban revolution will be] something in the range of eight months.

—CIA Director Allen Dulles as reported by the British Ambassador to the United State (1959)

I give Castro a year. No longer.

—Fulgencio Batista (Deposed Cuban President) (1959)

You just give me the word and I'll turn that fucking island into a parking lot.

—Secretary of State Alexander Haig to President Reagan (1981)

What's the point of my talking to him? All I'd tell him is what I'm telling you, to give the people the freedom that they want. And then you'll see the United States do exactly what we should: Go down and lift those people up.

—President George H. W. Bush (1982) about Fidel Castro

... hard as it may be to accept, our policy toward Cuba has failed and it is now time to change our focus from trying to destroy Cuba's government to helping its people.

—Former president Richard Nixon (1994)

I think our policy of sanctions against Cuba is ridiculous. During the cold war it made sense because it was a Russian base. They used it for flying spying missions, and so on, but that's over. And all we do by our sanctions is allow Castro, and now maybe his brother, to blame the problems of Cuba on us.[83]

—Former Reagan Secretary of State George Schultz (2008)

---

[83] www.thewashingtonnote.com/archives/2009/10/former_sec_of_s/

It is my personal belief that the Castros do not want to see an end to the embargo and do not want to see normalization with the United States, because they would lose all of their excuses for what hasn't happened in Cuba in the last 50 years. [84]

—*Secretary of State Hillary Clinton (2010)*

Dumbest policy on the face of the earth. It's crazy. [85]

—*Col. Lawrence Wilkerson (former chief of staff to US Sec. of State Colin Powell) on US policy towards Cuba (2006)*

One must first understand the following: The United States is to the Cuban government like al Qaeda is to Washington, only much more powerful and much closer. Since the Cuban revolution, the United States and anti-Castro Cuban exiles in the United States have inflicted upon Cuba greater damage and greater loss of life than what happened in New York and Washington on September 11, 2001.

—*William Blum (American author) (2007)*

---

[84] Reuters   http://reut.rs/U0vtvt

[85] www.gq.com/news-politics/newsmakers/200610/colin-powell-bush-administration?currentPage=7

Embargo

Although the US embargo of Cuba is an integral part of US-Cuban relations discussed in the chapter above, it is such a major factor that it deserves its own chapter. Despite all of the other harsh actions that the US government has taken against Cuba for more than fifty years, the embargo has been the most powerful and the most destructive to Cuban society and the life of everyday Cubans. It is condemned by almost every other country in the world and even by a large number of Americans. Yet it continues no matter who is president of the United States, and no matter which political party controls the US government.

Cubans refer to the US embargo as *el bloqueo* ("the blockade")

The American government prefers to call it an "embargo." In fact, it *is* a blockade, but without the gunboats. Trade is blocked with economic weapons, not guns.

The embargo of Cuba is an economic, commercial and financial blockade initiated by President Eisenhower, expanded by President Kennedy, codified into law by President Clinton, made stricter by President George W. Bush, and continued by President Obama.

Stages of the Embargo

All stages are cumulative, adding ever-harsher measures to the embargo.

1960 – Operation Pluto: US President Dwight Eisenhower cancels purchases of sugar from Cuba and shipments of oil to Cuba. Continues arms embargo begun the previous year. Later, Eisenhower imposes a blockade on everything except food and medicine.

1962 – President John Kennedy forbids any purchases from Cuba, denies access to US ports for ships that visit Cuba, and prohibits Americans from visiting Cuba.

1992 – Torricelli Act prohibits foreign subsidiaries of US corporations from trading with Cuba.

1996 – Helms-Burton Act prohibits foreign companies that trade with Cuba from trading with the United States.

2004 – President George W. Bush all but halts cultural, scientific, academic and sports exchanges between the United States and Cuba.

Cuba for the Misinformed

2009 – President Barack Obama eases travel restrictions on Cuban-Americans and allows some exchanges but renews blockade.

When the US government says the "international community" supports its economic embargo of Cuba, it means "Israel"

Every year for 21 years an overwhelming majority of countries at the United Nations has voted against the US embargo of Cuba. In 2012 the vote was 188-3 against the embargo.

Vote total at the United Nations General Assembly on 13 November 2012 calling for the United States to end its embargo of Cuba.
CREDIT: UNITED NATIONS NEWS CENTRE

Here is the complete list of countries who in 2012 voted to support the US embargo of Cuba:

> United States
> Israel
> Palau

Here is the complete list of countries who in 2012 voted against the embargo:

> Afghanistan, Albania, Algeria, Andorra, Angola, Antigua and Barbuda, Argentina, Armenia, Australia, Austria, Azerbaijan, Bahamas, Bahrain, Bangladesh, Barbados, Belarus, Belgium, Belize, Benin, Bhutan, Bolivia, Bosnia and Herzegovina, Botswana, Brazil, Brunei Darussalam, Bulgaria, Burkina Faso, Burundi, Cambodia, Cameroon, Canada, Cape Verde, Central African Republic, Chad, Chile, China, Colombia, Comoros, Congo, Costa Rica, Côte d'Ivoire, Croatia, Cuba, Cyprus, Czech Republic, Democratic People's Republic of Korea, Democratic Republic of the Congo, Denmark, Djibouti, Dominica, Dominican Republic, Ecuador, Egypt, El Salvador, Equatorial Guinea, Eritrea, Estonia, Ethiopia,

Fiji, Finland, France, Gabon, Gambia, Georgia, Germany, Ghana, Greece, Grenada, Guatemala, Guinea, Guinea-Bissau, Guyana, Haiti, Honduras, Hungary, Iceland, India, Indonesia, Iran, Iraq, Ireland, Italy, Jamaica, Japan, Jordan, Kazakhstan, Kenya, Kiribati, Kuwait, Kyrgyzstan, Lao People's Democratic Republic, Latvia, Lebanon, Lesotho, Liberia, Libya, Liechtenstein, Lithuania, Luxembourg, Madagascar, Malawi, Malaysia, Maldives, Mali, Malta, Mauritania, Mauritius, Mexico, Monaco, Mongolia, Montenegro, Morocco, Mozambique, Myanmar, Namibia, Nauru, Nepal, Netherlands, New Zealand, Nicaragua, Niger, Nigeria, Norway, Oman, Pakistan, Panama, Papua New Guinea, Paraguay, Peru, Philippines, Poland, Portugal, Qatar, Republic of Korea, Republic of Moldova, Romania, Russian Federation, Rwanda, Saint Kitts and Nevis, Saint Lucia, Saint Vincent and the Grenadines, Samoa, San Marino, Sao Tome and Principe, Saudi Arabia, Senegal, Serbia, Seychelles, Sierra Leone, Singapore, Slovakia, Slovenia, Solomon Islands, Somalia, South Africa, South Sudan, Spain, Sri Lanka, Sudan, Suriname, Swaziland, Sweden, Switzerland, Syria, Tajikistan, Thailand, The former Yugoslav Republic of Macedonia, Timor-Leste, Togo, Tonga, Trinidad and Tobago, Tunisia, Turkey, Turkmenistan, Tuvalu, Uganda, Ukraine, United Arab Emirates, United Kingdom, United Republic of Tanzania, Uruguay, Uzbekistan, Vanuatu, Venezuela, Viet Nam, Yemen, Zambia, Zimbabwe.

Abstain: Marshall Islands, Federated States of Micronesia

It is interesting to note that during speeches prior to the vote, when the Cuban representative finished speaking, there was a "resounding ovation." After the US representative spoke, "no one applauded," not even the representatives from Israel and Palau who would then vote *with* the United States. [86]

Here are comments on the embargo from people and organizations.

Dr. Benjamin Spock, well-known pediatrician and author of the huge best-seller *Baby and Child Care* wrote:

> I believe very few Americans realize what our country is trying to do down there—starve people into submission and deprive children and old people of medicine. [87]

---

[86] Chicago Tribune http://trib.in/T2FStV

[87] "Dr. Spock Takes Aid to Cuban Kids," *American Medical News*, February 22, 1993

Cuba for the Misinformed

Amnesty International has called for the blockade against Cuba to be lifted, stating that:

> It is highly detrimental to Cubans' enjoyment of a range of economic, social and cultural rights, such as food, health and sanitation—particularly affecting the weakest and most vulnerable members of the population...[and in sum]...is highly detrimental to Cubans' enjoyment of human rights.

> Seventy-four Cuban dissidents, including Cuba's best-known blogger, a hunger striker and the head of the Ladies in White protest group, have all called on the US government to lift the travel ban and remove restrictions between US and Cuban banks:

> We share the opinion that the isolation of the people of Cuba benefits the most inflexible interests of its government, while any opening serves to inform and empower the Cuban people and helps to further strengthen our civil society, [88]

On March 26, 2012, shortly before Pope Benedict VI's visit to Cuba, the Vatican stated:

> The Holy See believes that the embargo is something that makes the people suffer the consequences. It does not achieve the aim of the greater good," [and] "The Holy See does not believe it is a positive or useful measure.

The following month, on April 17, 2012, the US Catholic bishops' Committee on International Justice and Peace stated:

> All restrictions should be systematically examined and eliminated so that the complete abolition of the embargo and its harmful effects can be achieved. These burdens are not borne by the members of the Cuban governing elite, but rather by the 'ordinary' Cuban and especially by the weakest members of that society. [89]

A 2009 opinion poll conducted by *ABC News* and the *Washington Post* showed that 57 percent of Americans favor an end to the blockade (compared with 35 percent in 1998).

During the same period, a poll conducted by *CBS News* and the *New York Times* showed 67 percent of Americans favored re-establishment of diplomatic relations between the United States and Cuba.

---

[88] Seattle Times   http://bit.ly/SI1mx2

[89] www.news.va/en/news/us-bishops-call-for-end-to-cuba-embargo

Israel allows its citizens to visit (and invest in) Cuba whenever they wish

Despite Israel's support for the embargo at the United Nations, it fully supports its citizens going to Cuba even if Americans cannot. Thousands of Israelis go to Cuba each year on holiday. Israeli investors are also active in Cuba, constructing office and residential buildings, and controlling the world's largest citrus plantation under one management. This grove is over 115,000 acres (Gaza is only 88,000 acres) and is located near the Bay of Pigs in Jaguey Grande east of Havana. [90]

The US government says that Cuba uses the embargo as an excuse for its own bad policies

As Cuba points out, if the US government believes that Cuba really does have bad policies, why does that government not end the embargo and let the world see what happens once Cuba no longer has that excuse? [91]

Cuba has estimated its economic losses due to the US embargo at more than $89 billion

In the General Assembly report to the United Nations Secretary-General (2007) on the "Necessity of ending the economic, commercial and financial embargo imposed by the United States of America against Cuba," the Cuban government stated:

> Direct economic damage to the Cuban people as a result of the economic, commercial and financial embargo by the United States against Cuba is estimated at more than $89 billion. This figure does not include direct damage to national social and economic objectives by acts of sabotage and terrorism fomented, organized and financed from the United States. Nor does it include the value of products that could no longer be manufactured or the damage caused by the onerous credit terms imposed on Cuba. [92] [93]

That amount was updated by Cuba's Vice Foreign Minister Abelardo Moreno in September 2011. Moreno stated that the cost to Cuba of the embargo through December 2010 was estimated at $104 billion, and that taking into consideration the "extreme devaluation of the dollar against the price of gold

---

[90] http://fred.ifas.ufl.edu/cubanag/pdf/citrus1.pdf

[91] Cuba Embargo's Golden Anniversary - http://www.havanatimes.org/?p=61646

[92] http://www.undemocracy.com/generalassembly_62/meeting_38

[93] United Nations http://bit.ly/S2fT8s

on the international financial market during 2010, [it] would add up to nearly a trillion dollars." [94]

The US embargo of Cuba affects countries and businesses all over the world

The embargo has major economic effects on Cuba because its restrictions affect all other countries in the world. [95]

- No article with more than 10 percent Cuban components can enter the United States. For example, no Japanese product containing more than 10 percent nickel from Cuba can be exported to the United States.
- Cuba is not allowed to import *from anywhere in the world* a product containing more than 10 percent components from the United States.
- Vessels from any country that dock in a Cuban port are prohibited from entering the United States for 180 days.
- Cuba cannot open accounts in any banks in any country if those banks have operations in a subsidiary bank in the United States.

As an official in Cuba's Ministry of Foreign Affairs summarizes "The essential harm is that Cuba has been prevented from developing itself to its full potential. The blockade prevents us from having relations with the United States and it impedes us from interacting with the rest of the world under normal conditions." [96]

"70% of Cubans born under the Blockade"
CREDIT: MARSHALL SOULES

Cuba has also lost valuable access to medical equipment and medicines. Rather than purchase those items from its neighbor just 90 miles away, it

---

[94] Caricom News Network   http://bit.ly/SDMdtW

[95] www.havanatimes.org/?p=61646

[96] www.havanatimes.org/?p=61646

must buy them from countries throughout the world, incurring much greater transportation costs and higher prices, particularly when it is necessary for the selling companies to take circuitous measures to avoid violating—or being discovered to violate—US law.

"One minute of the blockade is equivalent to all of the x-rays needed by one polyclinic in a year"
CREDIT: MARSHALL SOULES

You can buy Coca-Cola in Cuba despite the American embargo

Cuba reportedly buys about $10 million worth of Coca-Cola every year. As the Coca-Cola corporation is based in Atlanta, Georgia, Cuba buys it from Mexico. Cubans get the good stuff, too. Mexican Coke is made with sugar, not high-fructose corn syrup.

Coca-Cola on Varadero Beach poster (1958).
CREDIT: COCA-COLA

A 13-year old Cuban boy was denied a prize because of the Americans' embargo

In October 2006, a thirteen-year-old Cuban boy, Raysel Sosa, was singled out and publicly humiliated during an awards ceremony for an international art contest, when the Japanese company Nikon denied him a digital camera awarded to the other winners because the camera contained more than 10 percent American components, and the prize would amount to a violation of the US blockade. Nikon gave the boy a painting set instead.

Despite the embargo, Cuba receives food from the United States

The United States is currently the second largest exporter of agricultural products (primarily livestock feed) to Cuba. (Brazil is first.) This appears to violate the embargo but the US government has made an exception due to heavy lobbying from the agricultural industry in the United States. This does not mean that there is *trade* between the United States and Cuba. There is no trade. Cuba is not allowed to sell anything in return in order to achieve some sort of balance of trade. In fact, there is no credit and Cuba must pay up front—with cash.

Cuba produces about half of the food it consumes. From 2002 to 2010 the United States was Cuba's largest source of imported food. Due to global economic conditions, Brazil (which is offering Cuba lower prices) is now the largest exporter of food to Cuba.

The United States exported $4 billion in farm products—mostly feed stuffs—to Cuba from 2002 to 2008. About 95 percent of the total included corn, wheat, soybeans and soybean meal. The largest US value-added [processed in some manner] product exported to Cuba is poultry. Other export items include pork, dry beans and processed foods. Smaller amounts of apples, pears and grapes are exported to Cuba. [97]

A number of US states benefit from this export trade to Cuba. They include California ($9.5 million annually–cotton, grains, fruit including table grapes, dairy, poultry and processed foods), Florida ($79 million), Louisiana ($240 million), Mississippi ($22 million), Oklahoma ($9.2 million–frozen broilers and turkeys, wheat, animal feeds and pork), Texas ($45 million–wheat, corn, animal feeds, poultry and cotton), and Virginia ($53 million). [98]

Since the bulk of US food imports to Cuba is livestock feed, the importation of actual food for humans from the US has never remotely approached the levels prior to the Torricelli Act. That act continues to negatively affect the

---

[97] http://westernfarmpress.com/government/expanded-us-farm-exports-cuba-horizon

[98] (2009 figures)http://westernfarmpress.com/government/expanded-us-farm-exports-cuba-horizon?page=3

health and well-being of all Cubans—in the name of "democracy building," according to the US government.

Even revolutionaries need a Coke break now and then.
CREDIT: ARCHIVAL

Recommended viewing—

Ten Reasons: A film about the Cuban Embargo
http://youtu.be/rjQsH7AG4WI

International Aid

If there is one phrase that captures the international spirit of the Cuban people, it is Jose Martí's statement "Patria es humanidad" which can be translated as "[Our] homeland is humanity." Martí's deeper meaning was that the land of our birth is that portion of humanity that we know best, where we are most at home, and where we can have the greatest influence. By serving our own immediate homeland, we can fulfill our duty to our greater homeland: the entire world and entire humanity. Cubans recognize that they are part of the world, part of something greater, and their concern and compassion for people of other countries is demonstrated by their actions.

Since its successful revolution, Cuba has been lending assistance to countries throughout the world, in particular helping developing countries trying to throw off the shackles of foreign government and corporate control.

For some years, Cuba did this with its military, most notably its assistance in Angola which helped defeat the South African army's invasion of that country, which in turn helped South Africans overthrow their apartheid government.

For some years now, Cuba's focus on international aid has been non-military; it exports teachers and doctors rather than soldiers and weapons. Cuba is not just a leader but the leader in providing health care around the world.

Cuba's incredibly successful literacy program, conducted in Cuba itself in 1961 to nearly eliminate illiteracy, has been exported to countries all over the world. Cuban literacy experts train people to become literacy teachers, so that the program can be tailored to their own countries by the Cuban-trained people of those countries.

Cuba's Latin American School of Medicine trains students from many different countries at no charge to become physicians. The only requirement is that those graduates return to their own countries to treat patients who currently have little, if any, access to health care. The school's students even include a number from the United States, who will return as fully-trained doctors to serve the medical needs of rural and poor areas.

In short, while the United States continue to send troops (and drones) into areas around the world, to establish bases in more than 150 countries, and to train Latin American military members at their now-renamed School of the Americas, Cuba sends doctors and teachers to poor and developing countries, and offers free medical school training to students from those same countries.

That is Cuba's expression of "Homeland is humanity."

Africa

Nelson Mandela thanked Cuba for helping end apartheid in South Africa

Nelson Mandela - former president of
South Africa (2008)
CREDIT: THE GOOD NEWS/WIKIMEDIA COMMONS

Nelson Mandela spoke out on October 6, 1995, about Cuba's participation fighting against South African forces in Angola's civil war:

> Cubans came to our region as doctors, teachers, soldiers, agricultural experts, but never as colonizers. They have shared the same trenches with us in the struggle against colonialism, underdevelopment, and apartheid. Hundreds of Cubans have given their lives, literally, in a struggle that was, first and

foremost, not theirs but ours. As Southern Africans we salute them. We vow never to forget this unparalleled example of selfless internationalism.

We wish also to record our indebtedness to Cuban hospitality. In particular, tens of thousands of young Southern Africans have been trained, and some are still training, in Cuban schools and universities. Today, in many different fields - in the health sector, in government, and in the army - there are many young professionals, contributing to the development of our country, who owe their skills to the generous training provided to them by Cuba.

Many people, many countries, including many powerful countries, have called upon us to condemn the suppression of human rights in Cuba.

We have reminded them they have a short memory.

For when we battled against apartheid, against racial oppression, the same countries were supporting the apartheid regime...And we fought successfully against that regime with the support of Cuba and other progressive countries.

They now want to be our only friends, and dare to ask us to renounce those people who made our victory possible. That is the greatest contempt for the morality and the principles which are the basis of our relations, not only with the various population groups in this country, but with the entire world.

And I wanted to make a commitment that we will never let our friends down, friends during the most difficult period of our struggle, especially Cuba. [99]

---

[99] NelsonMandela.org   http://bit.ly/U7vbc7

Cuba helped defeat the South African apartheid government's army

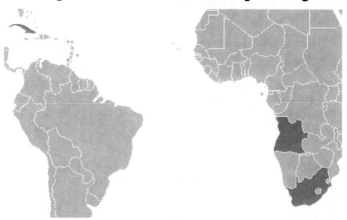

Military forces from Cuba (top left) traveled to Angola (lower west coast of Africa) to help that country defeat the army of apartheid South Africa (bottom of Africa)
CREDIT: WIKIPEDIA

In October 2003, US professor Noam Chomsky said the following about the 55,000 Cuban volunteers[100] who helped defeat South Africa-backed forces between 1975 and 1990 in Angola and Namibia:

> It's an astonishing achievement...[and] another reason why Cuba is hated [by imperialism]. Just the plain fact that black soldiers from Cuba were able to beat back a South African invasion of Angola sent shock waves throughout the continent. The black movements were inspired by it. The white South Africans were psychologically crushed by the fact that South African forces could be defeated by a black army. The United States was infuriated. If you look at the next couple of years, the terrorist attacks [by US-supported Cuban exiles] on Cuba got much worse. [101]

President Bill Clinton told South Africa it should sever relations with Cuba

Siphiwo Sobuwa, a South African who spent 15 years in prison because of his activities with the African National Congress, made the following statement about US President Bill Clinton:

---

[100] It should be noted that for a small country like Cuba to send a force of 55,000 troops would be the equivalent of the United States, with its much larger population, sending more than one million troops.

[101] www.chomsky.info/interviews/20031028.htm

He came here a couple years ago to visit Mandela and speak to our Parliament, and he told us South Africa should cut its ties to Cuba because Cuba was a bad government. Well, when we needed help during our liberation struggle, Cuba gave it. When we needed food, Cuba provided it. For someone who did not help our struggle to come now and ask us to distance ourselves from someone who did, that is very arrogant behavior. [102]

Recommended reading—

Cuban documents on history of Africa involvement:
National Security Archive   http://bit.ly/SDFQXF

Fidel Castro of Africa:
http://natna.wordpress.com/castro-of-africa/

Recommended viewing—

Fidel Castro in South Africa
http://youtu.be/4tNF0YkRQjM

Nelson Mandela on Fidel Castro
http://www.youtube.com/watch?v=fSx4v3EcCfl

Nelson Mandela meets Fidel Castro
http://youtu.be/2n8Ff_g2UXw

Literacy Programs

Cuba has exported its literacy program to more than 20 countries

Since the Cuba Literacy Campaign of 1961 (see page 188), Cuba has led the Caribbean, Central America and South America in literacy. In the fifty years since its own successful literacy campaign, Cuba has sent literacy teachers and advisers to more than twenty countries throughout the world, including Nicaragua, Venezuela, Brazil, Mexico, Canada, New Zealand, Argentina, Haiti, East Timor, Mozambique, Paraguay and South Africa. More than 6 million people have learned to read through this program, called "*Yo sí puedo*" ("Yes I can"). This includes more than 1.5 million in Venezuela and, in 2012, eighty Australian Aborigines in the small town of Wilcannia. [103]

---

[102] Mark Hertsgaard, "The eagle's shadow: Why America fascinates and infuriates the world," New York: Picador 2003

[103] Fox News http://bit.ly/VJW3us

100,000 Cubans volunteered to take the place of two murdered Cuban teachers

In 1981, when two Cuban literacy teachers were killed in Nicaragua by US-backed Contras, some 100,000 other Cubans volunteered to take their place.

In 2006 UNESCO awarded Cuba the King Sejong Literacy Prize

Cuba received the award for "working through an innovative literacy method with more than 15 countries to use literacy to advance individual and social potential."

Although several other countries also received the award, only Cuba received it for *assisting* other countries.

Ironically, the United Nations in 1965 had refused to distribute its own report on the success of the Literacy Campaign. Here is a quote from that report:

> The secret of the success of the campaign must be found in a very simple fact, one that is very old and foreign to all technical means: human relationships. It must be found in those intellectual, emotional and psychological chain reactions, which arise when relations are established between one human being and another. [104]

Chernobyl Victims

Cuba has treated thousands of victims of the 1986 nuclear disaster in Chernobyl

Since 1990 Cuba has treated more than 20,000 children (and 4,000 adults) from Ukraine and other Eastern European countries who were victims of the Chernobyl disaster in 1986, either directly or who were born later but affected by radiation.

More than 800 children a year, accompanied by adults, are treated at Ciudad de Pioneros Tarara, an oceanside medical facility outside of Havana. The children suffer from leukemia, thyroid cancer, vitiligo (a discoloration of the skin resulting from lack of pigmentation,) and hair loss. Many also have digestive and nervous disorders. Treatments can last anywhere from 45 days to a year, depending on the nature of the disorders.

---

[104] UNESCO – *Report on the method and means utilized in Cuba to eliminate illiteracy,*" July 6, 1965. p.73   http://bit.ly/TnLKMI

Ukraine pays for travel and incidental expenses, but the rest of the program, including the extensive medical costs, is borne by Cuba. Cuba provides more health care to these children than any other donor country in the world.

Cuban doctors in Ukraine select those children who would most benefit from the program. The US embargo has forced Cuba to limit the number and variety of children that it treats because the embargo has made it difficult and expensive for Cuba to obtain the drugs needed to treat leukemia and lymphomas with chemotherapy.

Website

Chernobyl – Cuban Humanitarian Program
http://www.sld.cu/sitios/chernobili/

Recommended viewing—

20 Years of Hope—http://youtu.be/P2kaXjq3cX0

Latin American School of Medicine (ELAM)

Cuba's international medical school trains students (including Americans) at no charge

Cuba has been providing social and medical relief to developing countries since 1969. After the devastation caused in Central America in 1998 by Hurricanes Mitch and George, Cuba made the decision to launch a medical facility that would train youths from Third World countries to become physicians in their own countries.

As a location they chose a former naval academy on the outskirts of Havana, turning that military complex into a medical complex. [105]

---

[105] An interesting note is that when the Americans and others forced the elected president, Jean-Bertrand Aristide to leave the country in February 2004, the 1,000 "peacekeeping" US Marines used Haiti's first and only public medical school in Port-au-Prince as their headquarters, turning that medical complex into a military complex. The school had only been dedicated two months earlier, and it was another six years before it was restored to its original peaceful purpose. *Revolutionary Doctors: How Venezuela and Cuba are changing the the world's conception of health care*, Monthly Review Press (2011), p. 195.

Cuba for the Misinformed

ELAM Medical school graduates
CREDIT: ELAM

Cuba's *Escuela Latinoamericana de Medicina*–ELAM (Latin American School of Medicine) now trains more than 10,000 students. Because of the needs of poor countries and poor areas of more developed countries, the training focuses on primary care, public health, and hands-on clinical experience.

The school currently educates students from Latin America, Africa, Asia, the Caribbean and North America. North American students since 2001 include some from the United States, usually from poor, underserved and rural areas. Those selected are given full scholarships which cover tuition, books, room and board, and a small monthly stipend. All that Cuba requires in return is that the students go back to their home countries and work in communities where medical personnel are greatly needed.

Presently students from twenty-eight countries attend the school, including more than 100 US students from twenty-three states, Washington, D.C. and Puerto Rico. As of July 2012, more than 15,000 students from 100 nations had become physicians since ELAM's first graduating class in 2005. [106]

During their training, all non-Spanish speaking students take an intensive Spanish course. Medical training takes six years, including two years of basic medical science, three years of clinical rotation, and a one-year internship. After the first two years at ELAM, students attend one of the twenty-one teaching hospitals located throughout Cuba.

In addition to standard medical training, students are also trained in disaster medicine, public health, and complementary and alternative medicine.

---

[106] Radio Cadena Agramonte   http://bit.ly/SEO17N

It is interesting to compare Cuba's Latin American school with the US government's school for Latin Americans, formerly known as the School of the Americas. (See School of the Americas p. 86)

Recommended viewing—

Latin American School of Medicine (in Spanish)
http://youtu.be/Us7m51aZF5k

A Walk in Cuba: Help Denied—http://youtu.be/-Owe9PNT3cs

US student at Latin American School of Medicine
http://youtu.be/4vo80heaBgg

US medical students in Cuba
Part 1: http://youtu.be/NIsn6_7vefc
Part 2: http://youtu.be/huSxjmdNpfs

Medical Care

Cuba provides more doctors to developing countries than does the World Health Organization

Cuba, a country of only 11 million people, has 28 medical schools to train top quality health professionals. Cuba shares some 30,000 doctors with Third World countries for free. In Haiti after the great earthquake, for instance, the first doctor 90 percent of the population had ever met was Cuban.

After the 2005 earthquake in Pakistan, Cuba sent 2,300 medical personnel to 44 areas of the country. The Cuban contingent was the largest medical group from any one country and was estimated to have saved 1,315 lives, set up 30 field hospitals, carried out 601,369 consultations, 5,925 surgeries and attended 125 births. [107]

Cuba created its international *Operación Milagro* (Operation Miracle) program in 2005 to help people with sight problems. In Bolivia alone, over a nine month period in 2008, the program performed 73,000 successful eye operations, all free of charge. [108]

Cuba is working to eliminate tuberculosis. In 2004, Cuba's rate was 6.6 per 100,000, which gives Cuba, along with Chile and Uruguay, the lowest rate in

---

[107] www.cuba-solidarity.org.uk/faq-answer.asp?faqid=13

[108] www.cuba-solidarity.org.uk/faq-answer.asp?faqid=13

Latin America. The goal is to reduce it to 5.0 or less. Over 100 of Cuba's 169 municipalities already have a rate lower than 5.0. [109]

Cuba gives adult tuberculosis patients 100 percent of their salary during treatment, and holds their jobs until the completion of treatment. The current recovery rate is more than 90 percent.

The US government entices Cuban doctors to stop treating Third World patients

The US government, through the Department of Homeland Security, offers incentives to Cuban medical personnel working in poor countries. It urges them to leave the valuable life-saving work they are doing in slums and rural areas and instead "defect" to the United States.

The Cuban government has paid to train these highly-skilled medical personnel and has been sending them since 1973 to poor countries throughout the world. These doctors, nurses and other professionals generally operate in areas where the country's own physicians do not wish to practice. In many cases, Cuba does this with no payment. In others, the Cuban government receives money or, as in the case from Venezuela, oil. As a result, the doctors receive a higher salary than they would in Cuba. The arrangement benefits both Cuba and the host countries as Cuba earns badly needed currency and the countries receive excellent medical services at a low cost. As of 2011, Cuba had more than 37,000 medical personnel in 77 countries. [110]

The US government is well aware of this medical aid to poor countries. On April 19, 2009 US President Barack Obama stated the following at a press conference following the fifth Summit of the Americas in Port of Spain, Trinidad and Tobago.

> One thing that I thought was interesting—and I knew this in a more abstract way but it was interesting in very specific terms—hearing from these leaders who when they spoke about Cuba talked very specifically about the thousands of doctors from Cuba that are dispersed all throughout the region, and upon which many of these countries heavily depend. And it's a reminder for us in the United States that if our only interaction with many of these countries is drug interdiction, if our only interaction is military, then we may not be developing the connections that can, over time, increase our influence and

---

[109] www.cuba-solidarity.org.uk/faq-answer.asp?faqid=13

[110] Wall Street Journal http://on.wsj.com/YBiCof

have—have a beneficial effect when we need to try to move policies that are of concern to us forward in the region. [111]

Almost three years earlier, on August 11, 2006 (under the George W. Bush administration), the Department of Homeland Security announced, in conjunction with the Department of State, that it would allow Cuban medical personnel conscripted to study or work in a third country under the direction of the Cuban government to enter the United States. This program is known as the Cuban Medical Professional Parole (CMPP) Program. [112]

Cuban medical professionals must be Cuban nationals or citizens, must be currently conscripted to study or work in a third country under the direction of the government of Cuba, and must not have any ineligibilities that would prevent admission into the United States.

These professionals include doctors, nurses, paramedics, physical therapists, lab technicians and sports trainers. The spouse and/or unmarried children accompanying the primary applicant in the third country may also be considered for parole at the same time.

In short, these "thousands of doctors from Cuba" are targeted by US government employees to forsake their humanitarian efforts and instead move to the United States. Although the program was initiated by the George W. Bush administration, Obama's administration has continued the policy.

According to the *Wall Street Journal*, through December 16, 2010, under this program 1,574 visas had been issued by US consulates in 65 countries. As the Journal says, this is still a small percentage of Cuban doctors sent overseas. [113] What the "defecting" doctors often do not know is that permanent residency and medical licensing in the United States are not guaranteed. Permanent residency can be prevented if the "refugee" had been a member of a Communist Party organization in Cuba. Since, in order to gain a medical degree and be able to work abroad, most physicians were required to join Cuba's Communist Youth Union, this can be a major obstacle. [114] They are also seldom informed of the difficulties—and expense—of taking and passing the medical licensing exam in the United States. As a result of all of these requirements, many recruited applicants are not able to get licensing or permanent residency. [115]

[111]   US State Dept. http://1.usa.gov/PNOJ40

[112]   www.state.gov/p/wha/rls/fs/2009/115414.htm

[113]   Wall Street Journal   http://on.wsj.com/YBiCof

[114]   http://www.cubagreenscreen.com/forum/showthread.php?tid=15250

[115]   www.huffingtonpost.com/sarah-stephens/cuba-doctors_b_1424736.html

Hurricane Katrina

The United States turned down medical aid from Cuba after Hurricane Katrina

Immediately after Hurricane Katrina struck, Cuba offered medical aid consisting of 1,600 medical personnel equipped with their own food and water (many with extensive overseas experience including helping tsunami victims, as well as hurricane victims in Cuba), field hospitals, and 83 tons of medical supplies. [116] More than a week later, while people in the New Orleans still desperately needed medical care, the US government finally responded by refusing the offer. [117] [118]

Undaunted, the Cuban government kept the brigade together, ready to takeoff on a few hours notice to help in emergencies anywhere in the world. [119]

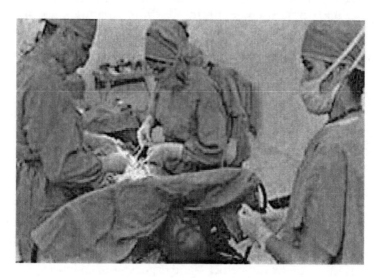

Doctors from the Henry Reeve Brigade – The brigade was rejected by the Bush administration when they volunteered to help Hurricane Katrina victims
CREDIT: RADIO REBELDE

Here is a description of the medical team that the United States rejected, as reported by Conner Gorry in *MEDICC Review.* [120]

---

[116] MSNBC http://nbcnews.to/Ry8FGH

[117] MSNBC http://nbcnews.to/YBlDoA

[118] Foreign Policy in Focus http://bit.ly/PNQ3UI

[119] www.walterlippmann.com/hurricane.html

Specialists in family medicine, cardiology, pediatrics, epidemiology and other fields, and trained in disaster response and the health risks engendered by such events, the health professionals were outfitted with two backpacks each, filled with 24 kilograms (52.8 pounds) of essential medicines. Resources carefully selected to provide maximum coverage for such a disaster, the backpacks contained re-hydration therapies, insulin, hypertension medications, treatments for systemic and topical infections, and minor surgical instruments, among others. With their packs on their backs and an average of 10 years clinical experience, these physicians were prepared to provide an experienced, mobile team able to move where health care was most needed. This flexibility would be enhanced by diagnostic kits carried by the doctors working alone or in pairs, for on-site patient evaluation in either English or Spanish.

The team as a whole already has considerable international experience, collectively having worked in 43 countries. They committed to stay in the disaster zone as long as necessary, as have many Cuban emergency medical teams before them.

- 857 are women; 729 are men.
- 699 have previously worked overseas.
- Average age is 32 years.
- Average clinical experience is 10 years.
- 1,097 are specialists in family medicine.
- 72 physicians have two or more specializations.
- All have disaster-preparedness training.

Recommended viewing—

A Walk in Cuba: Help Denied—http://youtu.be/-Owe9PNT3cs

Haiti Earthquake

Cubans were the first, and most effective, responders to the Haiti earthquake of 2010

When the 7.0 magnitude earthquake struck Haiti on January 12, 2010, Cuban health professionals were *already* in Haiti (they had been there since 1998), and were able to respond immediately to the disaster. Within hours they had set up field hospitals in the rubble—treating more than 2,000 people a day and a total of more than 25,000 survivors by January 26. As of March 23, they

---

[120] www.medicc.org/publications/medicc_review/0805/headlines-in-cuban-health.html

had treated 227,143 patients (more than the US, Canadian and Doctors Without Borders teams combined) and carried out 6,499 surgeries. [121]

The US government sent a 1,000 bed hospital ship—the *USNS Comfort*—which had a 550-person medical staff and remained in Haiti for only seven weeks. Over that time they treated 871 patients and performed 843 surgical procedures. [122]

The Cubans had a medical contingent approximately three times the size of the American medical group, yet the Cubans treated more than 260 times the number of Haitian patients than the Americans, and performed more than eight times the number of surgeries. [123]

It is interesting to note that more than 350 of the Cuban medical personnel were members of the Henry Reeve Medical Brigade, the same medical emergency organization that the Americans had rebuffed when Cuba offered their help to Hurricane Katrina victims in the United States in 2005.

Recommended viewing—

Cuban doctors help in Haiti—http://youtu.be/rk

---

[121] www.counterpunch.org/2010/04/01/cuban-medical-aid-to-haiti/

[122] www.counterpunch.org/2010/04/01/cuban-medical-aid-to-haiti/

[123] www.counterpunch.org/2010/04/01/cuban-medical-aid-to-haiti/

Government

Cuba's governmental structure is different from that of the United States, but Cubans consider it no less democratic. In fact, it can be argued that, in structure at least, it is more democratic.

Cuban government is pyramidal. At the base are the people themselves. Every two and a half years representatives to the Municipal Assemblies are chosen and elected by the people in their respective districts. At the time of voting, if no candidate wins a majority of the vote (not just a plurality), a second vote is held between the top two candidates. The winner then becomes a member of the area's Municipal Assembly, which can be compared to mayors and city councils in the United States.

Municipal Assemblies then nominate and vote for candidates every five years for the National Assembly. The Assemblies provide 50 percent of the members of the National Assembly; the other 50 percent comes out of various interest groups throughout the country, including workers' unions, women's groups, neighborhood associations (Committees for the Defense of the Revolution—CDR), students, youth and farmers. Members of the National Assembly are not paid, but they are given time off from their regular jobs to attend to their duties as assembly members.

The National Assembly in turn selects the 31-member Council of State, which in turn selects its top administrative officials.

When new bills are proposed, they are first discussed at the local level—the neighborhoods and CDRs. The results and recommendations move up to the Municipal Assemblies and after further discussion and suggestions, move up to the National Assembly, where they are discussed and approved.

The Cuban Constitution not only affirms the right to vote but a long list of other human rights. You can read these in the excerpts from the constitution provided.

Cuban Constitution

The Cuban Constitution states that the Communist Party is the "highest leading force of society"

Article 5 of the 1992 Constitution of the Republic of Cuba [124] states:

> The Communist Party of Cuba, a follower of Martí's ideas and of Marxism-Leninism, and the organized vanguard of the Cuban nation, is the highest leading force of society and of the state, which organizes and guides the common effort toward the goals of the construction of socialism and the progress toward a communist society.

The various articles of the Constitution, some of which are included here, must all be seen within the context of that "highest leading force." As Fidel Castro has said many times, "Inside the Revolution, everything; outside, nothing." [125]

The basic constitutional rights of Cubans include health care, education, employment and housing

> Article 9 includes these guarantees:
> – that every man or woman, who is able to work, have the opportunity to have a job with which to contribute to the good of society and to the satisfaction of individual needs;
> – that no disabled person be left without adequate mean of subsistence;
> – that no sick person be left without medical care;
> – that no child be left without schooling, food and clothing;
> – that no young person be left without the opportunity to study;
> – that no one be left without access to studies, culture and sports;
> – [that the state works to achieve] that no family be left without a comfortable place to live.

US Economic Bill of Rights

As an aside, it is interesting to note that US President Franklin D. Roosevelt proposed similar rights (in an "Economic Bill of Rights") for the American people in his State of the Union address to the US Congress on January 11, 1944. [126]

---

[124] http://en.wikisource.org/wiki/Constitution_of_Cuba

[125] www.worldaffairsjournal.org/article/cuban-days-inscrutable-nation

[126] http://www.fdrheritage.org/bill_of_rights.htm

These rights would have included:

- The right to a useful and remunerative job in the industries or shops or farms or mines of the nation;
- The right to earn enough to provide adequate food and clothing and recreation;
- The right of every farmer to raise and sell his products at a return which will give him and his family a decent living;
- The right of every businessman, large and small, to trade in an atmosphere of freedom from unfair competition and domination by monopolies at home or abroad;
- The right of every family to a decent home;
- The right to adequate medical care and the opportunity to achieve and enjoy good health;
- The right to adequate protection from the economic fears of old age, sickness, accident, and unemployment;
- The right to a good education.

These rights have been only partially implemented in the nearly seven decades since Roosevelt first proposed them.

Other sections of the Cuban Constitution include:

Article 35: The state protects the family, motherhood and matrimony. The state recognizes the family as the main nucleus of society and attributes to it the important responsibilities and functions in the education and formation of the new generations.

Article 37: All children have the same rights, regardless of being born in or out of wedlock.

Article 38: The parents have the duty to provide nourishment for their children; to help them to defend their legitimate interests and in the realization of their just aspirations; and to contribute actively to their education and integral development as useful and well-prepared citizens for life in a socialist society. It is the children's duty, in turn, to respect and help their parents.

Article 41: All citizens have equal rights and are subject to equal duties.

Article 42: Discrimination because of race, skin color, sex, national origin, religious beliefs and any other form of discrimination harmful to human dignity is forbidden and will be punished by law.
The institutions of the state educate everyone from the earliest possible age in the principle of equality among human beings.

Article 44: Women and men have the same rights in the economic, political, cultural and social fields, as well as in the family.
The state guarantees women the same opportunities and possibilities as men, in order to achieve woman's full participation in the development of the country.
The state organizes such institutions as children's day-care centers, semi-boarding schools and boarding schools, homes for the elderly and services to make it easier for the working family to carry out its responsibilities.
The state looks after women's health as well as that of their offspring, giving working women paid maternity leave before and after giving birth and temporary work options compatible with their maternal activities.

Article 52: Everyone has the right to physical education, sports and recreation.

Article 53: Citizens have freedom of speech and of the press *in keeping with the objectives of socialist society* [emphasis added by author].

Article 54: The rights to assembly, demonstration and association are exercised by workers, both manual and intellectual, peasants, women, students and other sectors of the working people, and they have the necessary means for this.

Article 55: The state, which recognizes, respects and guarantees freedom of conscience and of religion, also recognizes, respects and guarantees every citizen's freedom to change religious beliefs or to not have any, and to profess, within the framework of respect for the law, the religious belief of his preference.

Article 56: The home is inviolable. Nobody can enter the home of another against his will, except in those cases foreseen by law.

Article 57: Mail is inviolable. It can only be seized, opened and examined in cases prescribed by law. Secrecy is maintained on matters other than those which led to the examination. The same principle is to be applied in the case of cable, telegraph and telephone communications.

Elections

Cuban elections have high grassroots involvement

In Cuba, elections take place every two and a half years. The right to participate and to be heard is fixed in the Constitution, and Cubans have the opportunity to participate in decision-making both in their neighborhoods and their work places.

- Voting is secret and voluntary.
- Votes are counted publicly, with anyone (including the press) able to attend.
- There is universal suffrage for those 16 years of age and over.
- A candidate must be approved by an absolute majority (more than 50%) of the voters. If a candidate fails to receive this majority (this has never happened for the National Assembly), either the seat is left vacant or another candidate is selected in a by-election.
- Voters have the right to recall delegates.

Municipal Assembly

There are 169 municipalities in Cuba. Every two and a half years each municipality elects the members of its Municipal Assembly. Candidates are chosen through neighborhood meetings, and campaigning consists only of the distribution and posting of flyers, paid for by the state. Winning deputies then choose the municipalities' officers, the equivalents of mayor and other city council positions in the United States. Anybody can be nominated as a candidate for election.

While there are several parties, there is only one *official* party: the Communist Party of Cuba, which is estimated at some 800,000 members. Not even that party is allowed to participate in the election. It is not required to be a member of the Communist Party of Cuba to be elected to any position, although the vast majority of elected officials in Cuba are members. The party does not propose, support or elect candidates. Instead, individuals directly nominate those who they think should be candidates.

The nominations take place at urban and rural community meetings where residents select the nominees by raising their hands. The ballots will have two to eight names, and voters can choose only one of those candidates. A winning candidate must have more than 50 percent of the vote; otherwise, there is a runoff election.

National Assembly

The National Assembly is the country's unicameral legislature. Deputies are elected to the National Assembly every five years. Fifty percent of the candidates must be chosen by the Municipal Assemblies. The others are proposed by nominating assemblies comprised of representatives of workers, youth, women, students and farmers as well as members of the Committees for the Defense of the Revolution (the neighborhood organizations), after initial mass meetings.

The National Assembly is the country's highest legislative power and currently has 612 members, with each member representing 20,000 inhabitants. The Assembly meets two times each year for only a few days at a time. Members are not paid, although they do get time off from their regular jobs. It has been reported that 90 percent of the National Assembly members are members of the Communist Party and that "this body has managed to legislate for almost four decades without a single deputy ever voting to the contrary." [127]

Critics say this is because delegates are afraid to vote against motions made by assembly leaders, and the National Assembly simply "rubber stamps" everything it is told to approve. However, it could also be because all proposed laws that come to a vote in the National Assembly have already been thoroughly discussed and approved at the municipal level and, prior to that, even at the neighborhood level.

Councils

Members of the National Assembly elect the thirty-one members of the Council of State, which acts in legislative matters on behalf of the National Assembly between sessions. (As the National Assembly meets only a few days a year, the Council of State actually runs the country.) In the event of a presidential succession, the National Assembly elects the new president. This has happened only once—in 2008, after Fidel Castro announced that he would not stand for re-election. He was replaced as president by his brother, Raúl Castro.

There are no expensive political campaigns in Cuba

In fact, there are no campaigns at all. Nor is there a discussion of issues. The lack of campaigning means that there is no involvement of money as a factor. No one can buy an election. The lack of issue discussion means that there is no way of determining what a candidate thinks about the needs of the country and what actions the government should take.

All that a voter will see is a resume of each candidate's adult life. Each candidate had been proposed by a nomination committee and his or her selection for the ballot had been approved by the local Municipal Assembly.

In the 2013 election, everybody won

In the 2013 election, Cubans voted to elect 612 deputies of the National Assembly, and 1,269 delegates of the 15 provincial assemblies. There was a turnout of 90.88%; previous elections since 1976 had never been lower than 95%.

Every candidate on the ballot was elected. Not a single one failed to meet the 50%+ minimum. Although the Communist Party officially has no

---

[127] www.havanatimes.org/?p=73682

involvement in elections, it is reported that almost all of those elected (which was everyone) are members of the Communist Party.

Ballot boxes for elections in Cuba are "guarded" by children

The children are elementary school students, members of the José Martí Pioneer Organization. (The Pioneers replaced the Scout Association of Cuba whose membership was terminated by the World Scouting Conference after the revolution.)

At the polling locations the Pioneers serve in pairs, standing next to the ballot boxes for two-hour shifts. They also assist voters with disabilities. After voters place their ballot in the box, they are saluted by the children.

Cuban president Raùl Castro votes as a young pioneer watches over the ballot box.
CREDIT: GRANMA

Peace

Cuba ranks higher than the US on the Global Peace Index

The *Global Peace Index* (GPI) "gauges ongoing domestic and international conflict, safety and security in society and militarization" in 158 countries. The 2012 GPI ranks Cuba at 70th place with an overall index of 1.951. The United States is ranked lower, in 89th place with an index of 2.058. [128] The most peaceful country is Iceland (1.113), followed by Denmark (1.239).

The index is composed of twenty-three qualitative and quantitative indicators from respected sources, which combine internal and external factors ranging from a nation's level of military expenditure to its relations with neighboring countries and the level of respect for human rights.

These indicators were selected by an international panel of academics, business people, philanthropists and members of peace institutions. The GPI forms part of the Institute for Economics and Peace, a global think tank dedicated to research and education on relationship between economic development, business and peace. The GPI is collated and calculated by the *Economist Intelligence Unit* (whose parent organization publishes *The Economist* magazine), with whom the report is co-written.

---

[128] www.visionofhumanity.org/gpi-data/

Military

Cuba's military forces are smaller than four percent of the US military forces

Number of armed forces personnel:

Cuba – 58,000 (2010) [129]
USA – 1,452,939 (2012) [130]

The US military budget is 7,000 times greater than Cuba's

Military Expenditure (2009): [131]

Cuba – $91.8 million
USA – $679.6 billion

Per Capita Expenditure:

Cuba (2003) – $51 [132] (no recent statistics available)
USA (2011) – $2141 [133]

Billboards

Billboards in Cuba seldom advertise *products*

Billboards (*murales*) are everywhere in Cuba, but instead of advertising products, they are created by the government and promote the revolution, reminding people of their common obligations, their common goals, their hopes, and the reasons for their sacrifices. As with all advertising, however, when a message is repeated over and over, it may have an unconscious effect but is usually ignored.

---

[129] James Hackett (ed.), International Institute for Strategic Studies (3 February 2010). *The Military Balance 2010.* p.78-79

[130] http://siadapp.dmdc.osd.mil/personnel/MILITARY/ms0.pdf

[131] http://milexdata.sipri.org

[132] http://www.nationmaster.com/time.php?stat=mil_exp_dol_fig_percap-expenditures-dollar-figure-per-capita&country=cu-cuba

[133] http://en.wikipedia.org/wiki/List_of_countries_by_military_expenditures

"200 million children in the world will sleep in the streets today - None are Cuban."
CREDIT: DAN DELUCA/FLICKR

"En cada barrio, *revolución*" –
"In every neighborhood, revolution"
CDR slogan in a Havana neighborhood
CREDIT: MARSHALL SOULES

"As in [Playa] Girón - Homeland or Death"
CREDIT: MARSHALL SOULES

"Our homeland is Humanity" Simón Bolívar, José Martí,
Che Guevara
CREDIT: BEAT MUTTENZER/FLICKR

Recommended viewing—

Cuban Billboards—http://youtu.be/-SnKiNtYRsw

Hitchhiking

All Cuban government vehicles are required to give rides to hitchhikers

This is part of Cuba's support of shared transportation, including carpooling and hitchhiking.

Holidays

Cuba celebrates five official holidays

January 1 – The Triumph of the Revolution

The day of the victory of the revolution led by Fidel Castro in 1959—after Fulgencio Batista fled the night before—which established the present government in Cuba.

May 1 – Labor Day

July 26 – Commemoration of the assault on the Moncada garrison (Official name means "Day of the National Rebellion")

The date after which the revolutionary movement (M 26-7) was named. In the morning of July 26, 1953, some 160 men under the command of Fidel Castro attacked the Moncada army garrison in Santiago de Cuba, Cuba's second-largest city. Although this action failed, it is seen as the beginning of the Castro-led insurrection that expelled Fulgencio Batista. There are normally two or three days (July 25-27) of this public holiday.

October 10 – Independence Day

On this day in 1868, Carlos Manuel de Céspedes, "Father of the Homeland," gave freedom to his slaves and started the independence war against the Spanish colonial power, which led to the Ten Years' War.

December 25 – Christmas

For decades Christmas was a normal working day in revolutionary Cuba. The Christmas celebration (and the corresponding holiday) was reestablished in 1998 after Pope John Paul II visited Cuba.

Measurement

Cuba uses the metric system

Cuba uses the metric system, as do almost all other countries in the world. The only three who do not are Liberia, Myanmar and the United States.

Cuba uses the Celsius system

Cuba uses the Celsius system to measure temperature, as do almost all other countries in the world. The only three who do not are Belize, the Cayman Islands, and the United States.

National Anthem

La Bayamesa (The Bayamo Song) has been the national anthem of Cuba since 1902

The lyrics and music are by Perucho Figueredo. It was first performed during the Battle of Bayamo in 1868. Bayamo is the capital city of Bayamo Province.

Spanish lyrics

¡Al combate, corred, Bayameses!
Que la patria os contempla orgullosa
No temáis una muerte gloriosa
Que morir por la patria es vivir

En cadenas vivir es vivir
en afrenta y oprobio sumido
Del clarín escuchad el sonido
¡A las armas, valientes, corred!

English lyrics

Hasten to battle, men of Bayamo!
The motherland looks proudly to you
Do not fear a glorious death
Because to die for the fatherland is to live

To live in chains is to die
In dishonour and ignominy
Hear the call of the bugle
Hasten, brave ones, to arms!

Recommended viewing (and listening)—

La Bayamesa—http://youtu.be/-pb8KE3cYEU

Prisoners

Cuba has considerably fewer prisoners per population than does the United States

In May 2012, the Cuban government reported that there were 57,337 prisoners in Cuban prisons. Based on a population of approximately 11 million, that is approximately 521 prisoners per 100,000 population. The US currently has 730 prisoners per 100,000.[134]

The US has a total of approximately 2,666,880 prisoners and another 4.9 million on probation or parole. The US has more people in prison than any other country, including China and India, which each have populations over one billion, while the United States has approximately 313 million people. [135] The United States ranks top in the world. [136] Cuba's recently released statistics would place it in about fifth place (along with Russia.) China is 123rd and India is 212th.

Retirement

Men can retire at 65 and women at 60

Although the lifespan for both men and women is approximately the same, women in Cuba are able to retire five years earlier. Until 2009, retirement age had been 60 for men and 55 for women. The Cuban government realized that with changing demographics, there would by 2015 be more people leaving the workforce than entering it, and so increased the age of retirement for everyone.

---

[134] International Centre for Prison Studies   http://bit.ly/QdP4gq

[135] http://bjs.ojp.usdoj.gov/content/pub/pdf/cpus10.pdf

[136] International Centre for Prison Studies   http://bit.ly/QdP4gq

Unions

Every law and regulation of employment and the economy must be approved by the Cuban trade unions

Cuba currently has eighteen different national trade unions organized by their respective industries. Membership is voluntary, and the unions have no connection with the Communist Party or the government (nor are most unionists Communist Party members.)

The *Central de Trabajadores de Cuba* (CTC—Workers' Central Union of Cuba) meets every five years and consists of representatives from each of the national unions, elected by the membership of those unions.

Cuba's Labor Code establishes the right for unrestricted union activity to exist in every workplace and legally protects the right to unionize. Although industrial action is not banned, it has seldom been necessary as conflicts are usually settled through negotiation and collective bargaining.

Women's Rights

Cuba was the first country to sign the United Nations' Convention on the Elimination of All Forms of Discrimination Against Women (CEDAW)

Cuba also *ratified* the convention later in the same year—1980. The United States signed the convention in 1980—but *still* has not ratified it. Only six other countries have not signed and ratified it (Palau, Sudan, South Sudan, Tonga, Iran and Somalia.) [137]

The convention defines discrimination as:

> Any distinction, exclusion or restriction made on the basis of sex which has the effect or purpose of impairing or nullifying the recognition, enjoyment or exercise by women, irrespective of their marital status, on a basis of equality of men and women, of human rights and fundamental freedoms in the political, economic, social, cultural, civil or any other field.

Full rights for women are a basic precept of the Cuban Revolution

The Global Gender Gap Report 2011[138] from the World Economic Forum "reveals those countries that are role models in dividing their resources

---

[137] Wikipedia http://bit.ly/WjWUYF

[138] www3.weforum.org/docs/WEF_GenderGap_Report_2011.pdf

153

equitably between women and men, regardless of the overall level of those resources." The report covers 135 countries, the US in 17th place and Cuba close by in 20th place (the highest in Latin America and the Caribbean.)

According to the report:

> The United States shows no gap in educational attainment, with very high levels of literacy for both women and men and very high levels of women's enrolment in primary, secondary and tertiary education, with women outstripping men in tertiary-level education. The United States places 6th in the world in terms of economic participation and opportunity, the result of high rates of women's labour force participation and prominent numbers of women in legislative, senior official and managerial positions as well professional and technical worker positions. However, the perceived wage inequality for similar work remains high, placing the United States 68th in the world on this variable.
>
> Cuba's position is supported in particular by a high proportion of women among professional and technical workers (60 percent) and in parliament (43 percent.) Cuba also has very high levels of enrolment in primary, secondary and tertiary education for both women and men.

The basic perspective of the Cuban revolutionary government was that a fair, non-discriminatory society could not be created while women were still oppressed. In 1959 only 12 percent of the labor force were women, and few were professionals or technical workers.

One of the first things the new government did was to establish the *Federación de Mujeres Cubanas* (FMC—Federation of Cuban Women) in 1960. The FMC is a non-governmental organization with over 3 million members—80 percent of the entire adult female population. It is the largest mass organization in Cuba and the largest women's organization in Latin America.

Current statistics for women in Cuba include

- Female life expectancy: 80.08 years (male 75.46) [139]
- Female literate population: 99.8% [140]
- Female percentage of university graduates: 65% [141]

---

[139] www.indexmundi.com/cuba/demographics_profile.html

[140] www.tradingeconomics.com/cuba/literacy-rate-adult-female-percent-of-females-ages-15-and-above-wb-data.html

[141] http://womenandcuba.org/Documents/burkmsmagazine.pdf

- University places occupied by women: 57% [142]
- Women are guaranteed equal pay by law [143]

Cuba provides paid maternity leave

As part of the free national healthcare system, the Maternity Leave Bill of 1974 guarantees women a total of eighteen weeks' paid leave with an extra two weeks if birth is delayed. The bill also includes the option of an extended leave at 60 percent pay until the child is one year old, with the right to return to the same job at the end of the leave—an option which can be exercised by the mother or the father. The US is the only developed country, and one of only a handful of countries in the entire world, that does not require that working mothers receive paid leave.[144]

The Cuban government also subsidizes abortion and family planning, places a high value on pre-natal care and breastfeeding, and offers "maternity housing" to women before they give birth.

Abortions are available on request up to the tenth week of gestation

The following is from the United Nations Department of Economic and Social Affairs, Population Division:

Grounds on which abortion is permitted

- To save the life of the woman
- To preserve physical health
- To preserve mental health
- Rape or incest
- Foetal impairment
- Economic or social reasons

An abortion requires the consent of the pregnant woman. Abortion is available on request up to the tenth week of gestation through the national health system.

---

[142] http://sdonline.org/52/cuban-development-strategies-and-gender-relations/

[143] www.cuba-solidarity.org.uk/resources/WomenInCubareport.pdf p. 2

[144] Save The Children   http://bit.ly/RyaiUQ

Cuba for the Misinformed

An abortion is considered "illegal" if performed in disregard of health regulations established for the performance of abortion, and the person performing such an abortion is subject to imprisonment for a period of three months to one year. If the abortion is performed for profit or outside of official institutions or not performed by a physician, the possible punishment is increased to imprisonment for two to five years.

An abortion is also considered "illegal" when performed without the consent of the pregnant woman. A person who performs such an abortion is subject to two to five years' imprisonment, if the abortion is performed without force or violence, and to three to eight years' imprisonment if force or violence is employed.

If gestation is five weeks or less, menstrual regulation is employed. Women require no confirmation of pregnancy, and minors do not require parental consent for menstrual regulation to be performed. For abortions, gestation of ten to twelve weeks requires confirmation of pregnancy. The pregnant woman must be examined by a gynaecologist and must receive counselling from a social worker. Women under eighteen years of age must have parental consent. Women under sixteen require authorization by a medical committee. For an abortion performed in the second trimester, in addition to meeting the conditions for abortion in the first trimester, the case must be authorized by a committee of obstetricians, psychologists and social workers. [145]

Cuba has a large percentage of women in its national legislature

Forty-five percent of the members of Cuba's legislature are women. The US has less than half of that: 17.9 percent in the House of Representatives and 20 percent in the Senate, for a total in Congress of 18.3 percent.

Worldwide, Cuba ranks in 3rd place, with the United States at 80th place. [146]

Note: In the 2013 election, the percentage of women in the National Assembly rose to 48.9%. In Provincial Assemblies, the overall percentage of women became 50.5%.

---

[145] www.un.org/esa/population/publications/abortion/doc/cubasr1.doc

[146] www.ipu.org/wmn-e/classif.htm The US ranking of 80 may have changed slightly (perhaps as high as 75th) as there has been a slight increase since the 2012 election.

Society

Cuba is a mix of ancestry, cultures and religions. As a Spanish colony for centuries, there is a high percentage of Spanish heritage. As a former slave colony, there is also a large percentage of African heritage. Even more, it is a mixed-culture country. Europeans, West Africans, Chinese, Jews, North Africans and others provide a mix not only of race but of religion and other affinities. There are Catholics and atheists, Bahá'ís and Santeria, Protestants and Muslims, straights and gays. But more than anything, there are Cubans; working together to create a better and more creative society.

Ballet

The Cuban National Ballet is one of the world's leading ballet companies

Cuban National Ballet
CREDIT: NACIONAL BALLET DE CUBA

The ballet company was founded in 1948 by *prima ballerina assoluta* Alicia Alonso and she is still its active director. Since the revolution, it has been funded by the Cuban government and has performed in 60 countries.

157

Cuba for the Misinformed

Performances are accessible for most Cubans because ticket prices are subsidized by the government.

Gran Teatro de La Habana – Home of the Cuban National Ballet
CREDIT: PABLO TRINCADO (PABLO/T) / FLIKR/CREATIVE COMMONS

Website: www.balletcuba.cult.cu

Recommended viewing—

Cuban Ballet marks 60th anniversary—http://youtu.be/d6rUQg1Aw7I

Don Quixote – National Ballet of Cuba—http://youtu.be/gWLiyJ5C03g

Film

Two Cuban films have been nominated for Academy Awards

Strawberry and Chocolate was nominated in 1995 for Best Foreign Language Film.

Chico & Rita was nominated in 2012 for Best Animated Feature.

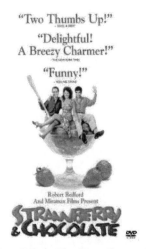

Poster for Cuban film Strawberry & Chocolate.
CREDIT: MIRAMAX FILMS

Cuba for the Misinformed

Poster for Cuban Film Chico & Rita.
CREDIT: FERNANDO TRUEBA PRODUCCIONES,
ESTUDIO MARISCAL AND MAGIC LIGHT PICTURES

Although not a Cuban-made film, *Buena Vista Social Club*—a movie about Cuban musicians directed by Wim Wenders—was nominated for Best Feature Documentary in 2000.

Recommended viewing—

Chico & Rita trailer—http://youtu.be/t82kD4oEoZU

Vampires in Havana is another popular Cuban animated film.

Poster for Cuban animated film
"Vampires in Havana"
CREDIT: CUBAN INSTITUTE OF CINEMATOGRAPHIC ART AND INDUSTRY

Juan of the Dead - A Cuban-Spanish movie released in 2012

Poster for Cuban horrorfun
zombie movie "Juan of the Dead"
CREDIT: THE ZANFOÑA PRODUCTIONS

Juan of the Dead trailer—http://youtu.be/Ff9rwB_B06U

Music

Ry Cooder, who produced the album "Buena Vista Social Club", was fined $25,000 by the US government for "trading with the enemy"

The album, which was recorded in 1996 and released in 1997, was a hit worldwide, leading to appearances by the musicians throughout the world and an award-winning documentary film by Wim Wenders.

The US government prosecuted Cooder because he traveled illegally to Cuba and spent money there, thereby breaking the Trading with the Enemy Act. He had entered Cuba via Mexico.

Although he was fined, he was able to return to Cuba legally for a further year of recording, thanks to an "act of clemency" from President Bill Clinton. [147]

---

[147] http://www.guardian.co.uk/music/2007/mar/04/jazz.popandrock

Cuban music is more than just the "Buena Vista Social Club"

Cuba has had a huge influence on music not just in Latin America but around the world, including the United States. Its music has transformed popular music since it was first popularized in the United States in the 1930s and 1940s. The worldwide album and movie hit "Buena Vista Social Club" exposed people in countries throughout the world to Cuban music. Cuba's legendary rhythms include son, bolero, danzón, mambo, rumba, cha-cha-cha, and now hip-hop. They are unique, exciting, and in most cases exceptionally danceable.

Street musicians in La Habana Vieja (Old Havana).

Here is further information from Wikipedia's "Music of Cuba" section: [148]

Son

> Son cubano is a style of music that originated in Cuba and gained worldwide popularity in the 1930s. Son combines the structure and elements of Spanish canción and the Spanish guitar with African rhythms and percussion instruments. Cuban son is one of the most influential and widespread forms of Latin American music: its derivatives and fusion, especially salsa, have spread across the world.

---

[148] http://en.wikipedia.org/wiki/Music_of_Cuba

Recommended viewing—

Classic Cuban Son—http://youtu.be/dgbpOy5v-AY

Bolero

Bolero is a genre of slow-tempo Latin music and its associated dance and song. The bolero is perhaps the first great Cuban musical and vocal synthesis to win universal recognition.

The Cuban bolero tradition originated in Santiago de Cuba in the last quarter of the 19th century; it does not owe its origin to the Spanish music and song of the same name. In the 19th century there grew up in Santiago de Cuba a group of itinerant musicians who moved around earning their living by singing and playing the guitar.

Recommended viewing—

Boleros of Cuba—http://youtu.be/ZUzgq35MnLY

Danzón

Danzón is an elegant musical form that was once more popular than the son in Cuba. It is a descendent of the creolized Cuban contradanza. The danzón marks the change from the communal sequence dance style of the late 18th century to the couple dances of later times. The stimulus for this was the success of the once-scandalous waltz, where couples danced facing each other, independently from other couples and not as part of a pre-set structure. The danzón was the first Cuban dance to adopt such methods, though there is a difference between the two dances. The waltz is a progressive ballroom dance where couples move round the floor in an anti-clockwise direction; the danzón is a 'pocket-handkerchief' dance where a couple stays within a small area of the floor.

Recommended viewing—

Traditional Cuban Danzón—http://youtu.be/RK-pLm1TxRI

Cuba for the Misinformed

Mambo

Mambo is a musical form and dance style that developed originally in Cuba and then later in Mexico. The word "mambo" means "conversation with the gods" in Kikongo, the language spoken by Central African slaves taken to Cuba.

Recommended viewing—

Cuban Mambo—http://youtu.be/Oqc1bAwMsrU

Cha-Cha-Cha

Cha-cha-chá is a genre of Cuban music. It has been a popular dance music which developed from the danzón in the early 1950s, and became widely popular throughout Cuba and Mexico, and in New York.

Recommended viewing—

Cuban Cha Cha Cha—http://youtu.be/NWrZXehnkAg

Rumba

Rumba is a family of percussive rhythms, song and dance that originated in Cuba as a combination of the musical traditions of Africans brought to Cuba as slaves and Spanish colonizers. The name derives from the Cuban Spanish word rumbo which means "party" or "spree." It is secular, with no religious connections.

Recommended viewing—

Cuban Rumba—http://youtu.be/JO2Wk0r9wac

Classic Afro Cuban Rumba Party—http://youtu.be/kIYyODRhrxl

Nueva Trova

Nueva trova is a movement in Cuban music that emerged around 1967/68 after the Cuban Revolution of 1959 and the consequent political and social changes.

Nueva trova has its roots in the traditional trova, but differs from it because its content is, in the widest sense, political. It combines traditional folk music idioms with "progressive" and often politicized lyrics. It is related to nueva canción in Latin America, especially in Puerto Rico and Venezuela. Some of the nueva trova musicians were also influenced by rock and pop of that time.

Nueva trova is defined by its connection with Castro's revolution, and by its lyrics, which attempt to escape the banalities of life by concentrating on socialism, injustice, sexism, colonialism, racism and similar issues.

Recommended viewing—

Pablo Milanes - *Yolanda*—http://youtu.be/X2gBXiz6wdA

Pablo Milanes - *Los Dias de Gloria*—http://youtu.be/uUVHA_CbKxl

Carlos Puebla - *Hasta Siempre*—http://youtu.be/Y8ynNRN_MxQ

Silvio Rodríguez - *Unicornio*—http://youtu.be/a81AGfl0JOY

Silvio Rodríguez - *Ojala*—http://youtu.be/u80ocuvZxmY

Carlos Varela - *Una Palabra*—http://youtu.be/a9Urj7-e_RA

Carlos Varela - *Luz*—http://youtu.be/9hUcHIMpGv8

Carlos Varela/Pablo Milanes – *Los Dias no Volveran*—http://youtu.be/fFhrV4osefk

Guantanamera

Popularized in the US by folk singer Pete Seeger, *Guantanamera* is the best-known Cuban song in the world

The music for Guantanamera was written in 1929 by Joseíto Fernández. His original lyrics had to do with a woman from Guantánamo. The lyrics used today were adapted from José Martí's poem "Versos Sencillos".

Spanish lyrics

Yo soy un hombre sincero
De donde crece la palma
Yo soy un hombre sincero
De donde crece la palma

Cuba for the Misinformed

Y antes de morirme quiero
Echar mis versos del alma

Guantanamera, guajira Guantanamera
Guantanamera, guajira Guantanamera

Mi verso es de un verde claro
Y de un carmin encenidido
Mi verso es de un verde claro
Y de un carmin encenidido
Mi verso es un cierro herido
Que busca en el monte amparo

Guantanamera, guajira Guantanamera
Guantanamera, guajira Guantanamera

Con los pobres de la tierra
Quiero yo mi suerte echar
Con los pobres de la tierra
Quiero yo mi suerte echar
El arroyo de la sierra
Me complace mas que el mar

English lyrics

I am a truthful man
From where the palm tree grows
And before dying I want
To let out the verses of my soul

My verse is light green
And it is flaming red
My verse is a wounded stag
Who seeks refuge on the mountain

I grow a white rose
In July just as in January
For the honest friend
Who gives me his open hand

With the poor people of the earth
I want to cast my lot
The brook of the mountains
Gives me more pleasure than the sea

Recommended viewing—

Pete Seeger – *Guantanamera*—http://youtu.be/X5JLCAIJLJ8

Chinese Cubans

Chinese first arrived in Cuba in the mid-1800s to labor in sugar cane plantations and the railroads

Over the years, most Chinese immigrants moved to Havana where they created the city's forty-four-square-block Chinatown. A small part of the area remains.

Gate of the Dragons - Chinatown's Main Gate in Havana.
CREDIT: DETZNAGA/WIKIMEDIA COMMONS

Today only a few hundred pure Chinese remain but there are many thousands of Cuban-Chinese throughout all areas of Cuban society. Several of the leaders of the Cuban Revolution were of Chinese descent and they continued to be in high leadership roles–both in politics and the military–in the post-Revolution decades. Armando Choy, Gustavo Chui, and Moisés Sío Wong, all fought in the revolution and were eventually promoted to the rank of general. Well-known Cuban artist Wilfredo Lam's father was a Chinese immigrant.

Recommended viewing—

Havana's "barrio chino"—http://youtu.be/qhjjtL0VEoQ

Jewish Cubans

Cuban Jews have total religious freedom

There are approximately 1,400 Jews in Cuba, with 1,100 in Havana and another 300 throughout the island. They have complete freedom to practice their religion, as do members of all other religions.

The leader of Havana's Sephardic synagogue says that, unlike other Latin American countries, Cuba has no anti-Semitism. She points out that there are no fences or guards outside Cuba's five synagogues, [149] three of which are in Havana. "We have our Jewish life with Cuban style. We do our services with heart," even though there hasn't been a full-time rabbi on the island since the early 1960s. [150]

The US government says "humanitarian tourist" Alan Gross is innocent, yet his wife and the leader of the main synagogue in Havana believe he broke Cuban laws

Alan Gross is an American currently in a Cuban military prison hospital in Havana (at the time of this book's publication.) In 2011 he was sentenced by Cuba to fifteen years in prison on charges that he acted "against the independence and territorial integrity of the state."

The US government claims that Gross is innocent and that he was simply carrying computers and various communications equipment in a humanitarian mission to help fellow Jews in Cuba connect to the Internet. Cuba says otherwise; that Gross was a spy helping to undermine the country and its government. Gross told the Cubans he was a tourist with a Jewish humanitarian group and never identified himself as working for the US government.

Gross had a $500,000 contract with Development Alternatives, Inc. (DAI) which "had a multimillion-dollar contract with USAID to break Cuba's information blockade by 'technological outreach through phone banks, satellite Internet and cell phones.' " [151] DAI in turn is funded by the US Agency for International Development (USAID) which is, in turn, overseen by the US Department of State. USAID in 2011 spent $20 million on its Cuban budget. [152]

---

[149] http://jewishcuba.org/synagogues.html

[150] www.jewishexponent.com/article/25904/Cuba_Extends_Welcome/

[151] www.businessweek.com/ap/financialnews/D9SSHGPG2.htm

[152] http://1.usa.gov/Xc1Gr6

Cuba's government considers all USAID activities in Cuba to be illegal and a threat to the country's national security. USAID denies that any of its work is covert. Mark Lopes, a deputy assistant administrator at USAID, says:

> Nothing about USAID's Cuba programs is covert or classified in any way. We simply carry out activities in a discreet manner to ensure the greatest possible safety of all those involved.[153]

Others disagree.

"Of course, this is covert work," said Robert Pastor, Director of the Center for Democracy and Election Management at American University in Washington and formerly President Jimmy Carter's national security adviser for Latin America. "It's about regime change." [154]

Although the US government says Gross is innocent, and Gross himself says he was a "trusting fool" who was duped (by whom he does not say), others say he probably knew what he was doing and that he absolutely knew he was breaking the laws of Cuba.

The leader of Havana's Sephardic synagogue says that Gross "broke Cuban laws," and added that members of the Jewish community now visit Gross "from time to time." [155]

Gross's wife Judy has stated, "We know now that he did break Cuban law. He did not know that until he got to Cuba and was arrested." [156]

Gross himself warned in one of his reports back to the government that "detection of satellite signals will be catastrophic." In another memo he wrote, "This is very risky business." [157]

It is relevant to note that the Helms-Burton Act passed by the US Congress in 1996 includes the following in Section 109: [158]

> (a) Authorization...the President is authorized to furnish assistance and provide other support for individuals and independent nongovernmental organizations to support democracy-building efforts for Cuba.

The Helms-Burton act is the authority for the funding of USAID's Cuban program. Its goal is regime change in Cuba, although the US government

---

[153] www.businessweek.com/ap/financialnews/D9SSHGPG2.htm

[154] www.businessweek.com/ap/financialnews/D9SSHGPG2.htm

[155] www.jewishexponent.com/article/25904/Cuba_Extends_Welcome/

[156] CBS Baltimore http://cbsloc.al/QdNzyE

[157] http://www.businessweek.com/ap/financialnews/D9SSHGPG2.htm

[158] www.state.gov/www/regions/wha/cuba/helms-burton-act.html

refers to it as "democracy-building." Part of that democracy-building is to make sure that Cuba is "substantially moving toward a market-oriented economic system based on the right to own and enjoy property." [159]

Another goal is "to strengthen international sanctions against the Castro government." Another demands that Cuba's new government "does not include Fidel Castro or Raúl Castro." [160]

Gross made five visits to Cuba during 2009. On the fifth visit, he was arrested. When arrested, he possessed "a specialized mobile phone chip that experts say is often used by the Pentagon and the CIA (and, apparently, the State Department) to make satellite signals virtually impossible to track." [161] This would likely be a "Discrete Operation SIM" which disables position reporting so that the phone can be tracked to an area no smaller than 200-600 kilometers in diameter. [162] The chip is reportedly not available on the open market.

Much of the other equipment Gross helped bring in is legal in Cuba, but the volume of equipment could have easily made Cuban authorities suspicious.

The equipment he brought into Cuba on his fourth trip included: twelve iPods, eleven BlackBerry Curve smartphones, three MacBooks, six 500-gigabyte external drives, three Internet satellite phones known as BGANs (Broadband Global Area Network), three routers, three controllers, eighteen wireless access points, thirteen memory sticks, three phones to make calls over the Internet, and networking switches. The satellite phones and networking equipment are explicitly forbidden in Cuba.

When traveling to Cuba, Gross asked fellow American Jewish passengers to take electronic equipment for him in their carry-on luggage, and then to return it to him later at his hotel in Cuba. [163]

The BGANs were important because they allowed users to connect to the Internet via satellite without going through government-controlled servers. [164] Gross wrote that he smuggled the satellite phones in a backpack, hoping to fool authorities by taping over any identifying words on the equipment.

Gross traveled to Cuba under the guise of being with Jewish groups, who frequently visit Cuba. These groups generally bring medications, sundries, religious items and kosher food. (According to Jeffrey Goldberg in *The*

---

[159] www.state.gov/www/regions/wha/cuba/helms-burton-act.html - Section 206

[160] www.state.gov/www/regions/wha/cuba/helms-burton-act.html

[161] Huffington Post http://huff.to/Pu6e8d

[162] www.deltawavecomm.com/Files/BGAN/bgangov.ppt

[163] http://forward.com/articles/151432/what-did-alan-gross-do-in-cuba/

[164] www.businessweek.com/ap/financialnews/D9SSHGPG2.htm

Atlantic, "They receive delegations of Jews from the US, Canada, Mexico and elsewhere almost weekly. When I was in Havana in 2010, the president of the Jewish community, Adela Dworin complained to me that she has a warehouse brimming over with cans of gefilte fish brought by well-meaning Jewish delegations.") [165]

The Cuban Jewish community never asked for Gross' help because they did not need it. They already had their own intranet as well as Internet access and had no need for the sophisticated equipment that Gross apparently brought in. Dworin denies any knowledge of Gross and says that recognized international Jewish organizations have provided them with legal Internet connections. [166]

USAID has not said why it thought the community needed such sensitive technology. [167]

More than 400 Cuban Jews secretly emigrated to Israel in the 1990s under *Operation Cigar*

In the early 1990s, Operation Cigar,[168] [169] a joint Cuban, Canadian and Israeli government operation, was launched. Over a period of five years, more than four hundred Cuban Jews secretly emigrated to Israel. The details surrounding the operation are unclear; some claim Margarita Zapata, a relative of one of Castro's close colleagues, convinced Castro to permit the Jews to emigrate. Castro did not want to publicize the emigration because it might appear he was allowing special arrangements to be made for Cuba's Jews. While, officially, all Cubans are allowed to emigrate, most do not have the finances to do so.

The first group of Cuban Jews, seventy in number, arrived in Israel in 1994. The Jewish Agency for Israel, an Israeli quasi-government organization which assists Jews worldwide who wish to emigrate to Israel, eventually covered the initial exit fee of $150, which was more than fifteen times the average monthly wage in Cuba.

---

[165] www.theatlantic.com/international/archive/2012/02/our-man-in-havana-or-the-strange-case-of-alan-gross/253025/

[166] CBS News http://cbsn.ws/Pu6kww

[167] www.businessweek.com/ap/financialnews/D9SSHGPG2.htm

[168] Wall Street Journal http://on.wsj.com/X99KZ0

[169] www1.jafi.org.il/papers/1999/oct/jtaoct12.htm

Patronato Vedado Synagogue, Havana, Cuba.

Freemasons

Cuba has two Masonic lodges for women

Although Masonic lodges in most countries admit only men; in Cuba, which has a number of male Masonic lodges, there are also two women's Masonic lodges: *Venus* in Havana and *Victoria* in the province of Pinar del Rio in western Cuba. More than sixty women belong to the lodges, and they range in age from eighteen to over sixty. Masonry in Cuba dates back to 1859, and Cuba's great national hero José Martí was a Mason.

Gays

Homosexuality was legalized in Cuba in 1979

There are no sanctions against homosexuality, which has been legal since 1979. Currently a law is being debated which would allow legal recognition of same-sex unions, granting them the same rights as heterosexual couples.

Much of the credit for this change goes to the National Center for Sex Education (CENESEX), a government-funded organization formed in 1989 and headed by Mariela Castro, daughter of current President Raúl Castro.

The International Day Against Homophobia is celebrated on May 17th every year and includes conferences, discussions, debates and films. At other times, LGBT events and marches take place freely and regularly.

The Global Fund praised Cuba's approach to sexual rights

In its report to the United Nations' Secretary-General on the US embargo of Cuba, the Global Fund to Fight AIDS, Tuberculosis and Malaria stated:

> The programs for men who have sex with men (MSM) supported by the Global Fund have a broad spectrum of activities with foci on the promotion of human rights and the respect of sexual diversity. The program has significantly decreased the stigmatization of homosexuality in Cuban society and has stimulated a social and political dialogue on sexual rights that is unprecedented in Latin America. [170]

Fidel Castro admits homosexuals were treated unjustly

Although legalized in 1979, Cuba had traditionally discriminated against homosexuals. In the 1960s and 1970s, because of the HIV/AIDS epidemic, many were fired, imprisoned or sent to "re-education" camps. [171] As Fidel Castro has said, "Yes, there were moments of great injustice—great injustice." While Castro has stated that he personally has no such prejudice, and that during those years his focus was on protecting the country—primarily from attacks and sabotage by the Americans and the CIA—he should have paid more attention to what was happening to the gay community. "If anyone has to take responsibility, I take mine. I will not hold anyone else responsible." [172]

The re-education camps were not as harsh as they sounded. Their purpose was to provide treatment—and a comfortable death—for those with AIDS, and to keep them from infecting others. Patients were fed and housed, given medical treatment, received the salaries they had previously been earning, and could attend a variety of education and art classes. After some years the camps were turned into sanitariums and restrictions were gradually lessened. Out of the original fourteen, there are now only three sanitariums left, each with considerably smaller populations than they once had. Those patients who remain do so because they choose to, since most treatment has been on an outpatient basis since 1993. [173]

Recommended viewing—

Gay rights in Cuba—http://youtu.be/yh2rx021XL0

---

[170] http://bit.ly/XG9e4S

[171] http://www.bbc.co.uk/news/world-latin-america-11147157

[172] The Telegraph http://bit.ly/PNNQbV

[173] http://www.nytimes.com/2012/05/08/health/cubas-aids-sanitariums-fortresses-against-a-viral-foe.html

Hurricanes

Cubans regularly experience major hurricanes—and are prepared

Cuba has a tropical climate that is moderated by the surrounding waters of the Atlantic and the Caribbean. The warm waters, however, also cause Cuba to be hit by frequent hurricanes.

Since Cuba has almost yearly experience with major hurricanes, it is extremely well-prepared to deal with them. Neighbors are trained to work together to prepare or, if necessary, evacuate. Because neighborhoods have their own resident medical personnel, those medical specialists know the needs of all their patients and which medications might be needed during a hurricane and possible evacuation.

The medical teams evacuate with their neighbors to shelters previously stocked with food, water, medical and other emergency supplies. No one would ever need to go to a stadium or other huge similar location such as those used in New Orleans during the Katrina disaster. All forms of transport are used to evacuate the residents, from cars, trucks and buses to helicopters and horse carts.

Household pets are also evacuated and veterinarians await those pets at the shelters. Evacuees even bring television sets and small refrigerators if they have concerns about the security of those items when they have left their homes. In rural areas livestock is moved to safe areas, and if there is time, crops are harvested.

Cuba does not wait until a hurricane is looming to prepare. All adults receive civil defense training, and children learn disaster preparedness starting in grade school. Every May, prior to the hurricane season—which begins on the first day of June—the entire country holds a two-day hurricane drill.

The US and Cuba work closely together to monitor hurricanes in the Caribbean area

Meteorologists from the two countries have worked together for decades tracking hurricanes and tropical storms. They share data, Cuban meteorologists have received special training in the United States, and Cuba allows US Air Force planes to enter Cuban airspace to track and measure storms.

Recommended viewing—

Beating the hurricane: How are Cubans prepared to face hurricanes?
http://youtu.be/yN9D-QmIwko

Internet

The US Government has blocked Cuba from having a fast broadband connection to the Internet

Cubans have not had good access to the Internet. One reason is the lack of computer equipment. Through its embargo, the US government forbids any equipment with any US components or software being sold by any country to Cuba.

The second problem for Cuba has been its lack of a good connection to the Internet. Because the US government has not allowed any underwater cable connection to Cuba, the country has had to rely on slow and expensive satellite connections. This lack of bandwidth is the major reason—or at least the major excuse—for most Cubans not having been given access to the Internet.

Venezuela has recently completed construction of a 1600-kilometer undersea fiber optic cable connecting Cuba to the Internet and to South America. [174] It was expected that after this project's completion, Cubans would have much greater access to the Internet. This has not yet happened. One indication of problems is that, as this book was being completed, the minister in charge of the country's communication system was fired, and replaced by his deputy.

National Drinks

Cuba is the birthplace of some of Americans' favorite rum drinks

Rum is a distilled beverage made from sugarcane, either directly from sugarcane juice or from molasses. Havana Club Rum, produced in Cuba, is distributed worldwide in more than 120 countries by the French company Pernod Ricard.

The United States is not one of those countries. The US government does not allow Havana Club Rum to be sold, largely because of the efforts of Bacardi, which produces rum in Bermuda (and produced it in Havana until 1959). Bacardi happens to be the largest single contributor to the political campaigns of Florida's staunchly anti-Castro Cuban-American members of Congress. Bacardi claims it owns the rights to the trademark "Havana Club" for rum in the United States because Cuba has not defended its trademark. The reason Cuba has not defended it is because it is not allowed to defend it—because the US government does not allow it to be sold in the United States, primarily because of Bacardi's lobbying (and funding) efforts.

---

[174] www.submarinecablemap.com/

Havana Club's finest rum is its *Máximo Extra Añejo* which retails for approximately US $2,000 a bottle (again, not in the United States). Fortunately the company's other rums are cheaper, with prices as low as $30.

Drink recipes courtesy of Pernot Ricard/Havana Club.
Website: www.havana-club.com

Cuba Libre

"Cuba Libre" was the battle cry of the Cuban Liberation Army during the war of independence that ended in 1899. American troops introduced Coca-Cola to the island in 1900 and soon Cubans were mixing cola with their rums and toasting "Cuba Libre" which means "free Cuba."

Ingredients

- Few drops of lime or lemon juice
- 50 ml of *Havana Club Añejo Especial* or comparable dark/golden aged rum
- 120 ml of Cola

Directions

1. Place two or three ice cubes in a tall glass.
2. Add the rum and lime or lemon juice.
3. Top with fresh cola and garnish with a slice of lemon or lime.

Daiquiri

The Daiquiri was invented at the beginning of the 20th century and named after the Cuban village of Daiquiri where local youths were looking for an original way to refresh themselves. Later, in the 1920s, bartenders from the famous Floridita improved the original recipe by using crushed ice and maraschino liqueur, giving the drink its fabulous and snowy aspect.

Ingredients

- 2 tablespoons of sugar
- Juice of half a lime
- Dash of maraschino
- 50 ml of *Havana Club Añejo 3 Años* (or comparable aged white rum)

Directions

1. Combine all the ingredients with crushed ice in an electric blender and serve.

Tip: To measure the right amount of ice needed for one drink, fill your glass fully with crushed ice, then add the ice to the blender.

Daiquiri Natural

The above is the recipe for a frozen Daiquiri as invented at *El Floridita* in Havana. A Daiquiri Natural does not use the maraschino and instead of crushed ice it is shaken over ice cubes and then poured into a cocktail glass.

Mojito

The mojito's name may come from *mojo*, a Cuban seasoning made from lime and used to flavor dishes. Perhaps as a reference to its lime ingredient, the drink became known as the cocktail with "a little mojo" (*mojito*).

Ingredients

- Two teaspoons of sugar
- Juice of half a lime
- Two fresh mint sprigs
- 50 ml of *Havana Club Añejo 3 Años* (or comparable aged white rum)
- Sparkling water

Directions

1. In a tall glass, gently crush the fresh mint (preferably with a "muddler—a wood or plastic bartender's tool to grind or mash ingredients such as fruit or mint leaves,")
2. Add the lime juice and sugar.
3. Add the rum and three or four ice cubes.
4. Top with sparkling water (a 2:1 ratio to the rum) stir
5. Garnish with a sprig of mint.

Recommended viewing—

Havana Club – Cuban Mojito Recipe—http://youtu.be/LYCR6eFd2V0

Guayabera

The *guayabera* is Cuba's official formal dress garment

Officials at state functions are required to wear Cuba's traditional shirt. Men must wear white guayaberas, with long sleeves, four pockets in front, and two pleats both front and back. [175] Women's versions can vary in color and style. The shirts are made of cotton or linen and are worn untucked. The government resolution requiring their wear stated: "The guayabera has been a part of the history of our country for a long time and constitutes one of the most authentic and legitimate expressions of Cubanism."

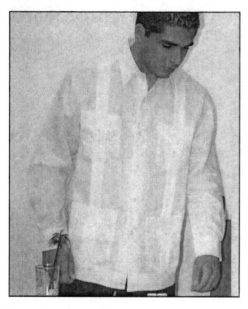

Long-sleeve guayabera
CREDIT: CUBANFOODMARKET.COM

Cubans claim that the guayabera first appears in the early 1700s on the banks of the Yayabo River in the central province of Sancti Spiritus. Depending on the version of the legend, the pockets were to hold either cigars or guava. Another theory is that the shirt originated much earlier in Mexico's Yucatan peninsula. Today the shirt is also common in Mexico, Puerto Rico, southern Florida, and the Philippines.

---

[175] www.bbc.co.uk/news/11492327

Neighborhoods

Every neighborhood in Cuba has an organization formed by neighbors to support each other

Comités de Defensa de la Revolución (CDRs—Committees for the Defense of the Revolution) are voluntary neighborhood organizations, financed by dues from their members. They are not government agencies, but the chairperson of each CDR is responsible for passing on the concerns of its members to the respective member of Cuba's Legislative Assembly.

Sign for a local Committee for the Defense of the Revolution (CDR).
CREDIT: DAVID SHANKBONE / WIKIMEDIA COMMONS

The CDRs were founded in 1960, and currently have eight million members in 122,000 chapters. They are usually composed of 50 to 100 families, and cover a block or two of a city, or a larger section of rural areas.

Their initial purpose was to protect their communities from attacks by the US and supporters of former Cuban president Fulgencio Batista. As Fidel Castro said, when the committees were launched:

> In the face of the imperialist aggression, we're going to implement a system of collective vigilance, so that everybody knows who lives on the block, what they do, and what relations they have with the tyranny, and with whom they meet.[176]

From a North American perspective, they are similar to a combination of a block watch committee, community center and neighborhood enhancement project. Their activities include regular monthly meetings, parties,

---

[176] CNN   http://bit.ly/Yl7Gw2

community gardens, recycling, immunization campaigns, blood drives, recreation, child care and neighborhood cleanup.

Obviously, particularly because the reason the CDRs were founded was to protect the then-recent success of the revolution, they can also be seen as tools of the government, watching for any deviation of loyalty to the state. Many Cubans do see this as the case, but some also see such vigilance as a necessity. As one Cuban said, referring to the ever-present enemy just ninety miles away, "If we have to act, we are going to act. Our streets cannot belong to criminals, or to counterrevolutionaries. The [US] Empire has the FBI; the Revolution has its CDRs."[177]

Recommended viewing—

Cuba's neighborhood watches: 50 years of eyes, ears
http://youtu.be/d-_WzI8D89M

Race

The majority of Cubans are dark-skinned

As many as 70 percent of Cubans living in Cuba are black or mulatto. (The US State Department says 62 percent, Cuban scholars say as much as 72 percent. Some Cubans believe it is 100 percent.) Non-white Cubans were the segment of the Cuban population least served by the Batista government and they have generally been the most supportive of the revolutionary government.

There are approximately 1.5 million Cubans living in the United States, two-thirds of them in Florida.[178] In the 2004 Census, 86 percent of them self-reported as being white. This is almost three times the percentage of white Cubans living in Cuba. It is obvious that, racially speaking, Cubans in southern Florida are not representative of Cubans in Cuba.

---

[177] AFP   http://bit.ly/Ts9wF3

[178] *Cubans in the United States*, fact sheet, Pew Hispanic Center, August 25, 2006, http://pewhispanic.org/files/factsheets/23.pdf

Cuban school children
CREDIT: GLOBAL EXCHANGE

Discrimination by race is illegal in Cuba but that does not mean there is no discrimination in the minds of some Cubans. Blacks and mulattoes may make up the majority of Cubans, but Hispanic (white) Cubans are in the majority of political power. Because most Cubans who fled Cuba after the revolution (and later) have been white, the vast majority of people in Cuba who receive remittances of money from their overseas relatives are white. This also means that the majority who receive gifts of electronics, food and clothing brought by their Cuban-American relatives on visits from the US are also white. In turn, this means a greater percentage of white than black or mulatto Cubans are able to use foreign currency given to them by overseas relatives which allows them to shop in hard-currency stores.

Religion

Sixty to eighty-five percent of Cubans consider themselves Catholic— and as many as eighty percent are followers of Santería

Cuba's constitution guarantees freedom of religion. All religions are welcome in Cuba, and the country has a variety of them. The most common is Santería, the Afro-Cuban mix of Yoruba (from West Africa) and Catholicism. African deities blend with Catholic saints to become beings that both religions can be relatively comfortable with. As the CIA Factbook states:

> Santeria: practiced in Cuba, the merging of the Yoruba religion of Nigeria with Roman Catholicism and native Indian traditions. Its practitioners believe that each person has a

destiny and eventually transcends to merge with the divine creator and source of all energy, Olorun.[179]

As Santería is, since the Revolution, both allowed and predominant, followers tend to emphasize the original African religion with reverence toward the *orishas* (Yoruba deities). These religious practices are commonly intermingled with Catholicism, and some even require Catholic baptism for full initiation, making it difficult to estimate accurately total membership of these syncretistic groups. Some sources estimate that as much as 80 percent of the population consults with practitioners of Santería.

Cuba's other religions include Catholicism, other Christian religions, Judaism, and Buddhism.

The US Department of State's July-December, *2010 International Religious Freedom Report* states the following: [180]

> The Roman Catholic Church estimates that 60 to 70 percent of the population is Catholic. [The CIA Factbook states that as many as 85 percent of Cubans are nominally Catholic.] Membership in Protestant churches is estimated at 5 percent of the population and includes Baptists, Pentecostals, Jehovah's Witnesses, Seventh-day Adventists, Methodists, Presbyterians, Anglicans, Lutherans, and the Religious Society of Friends (Quakers.) Other groups include Greek Orthodox, Russian Orthodox, Muslims, Jews, Buddhists, Bahais, and members of The Church of Jesus Christ of Latter-day Saints (Mormons).

> Catholic Church officials estimated that its membership was seven to eight million persons but that only 4- to 5-percent of baptized Catholics regularly attended Mass, while membership in Protestant churches was estimated at 600,000 to 800,000. Baptists, represented in four different conventions, and Pentecostal churches, particularly the Assemblies of God, are probably the largest Protestant denominations. The Assemblies of God reported more than 100,000 members; Jehovah's Witnesses reported approximately 92,000 members; Seventh-day Adventists and Methodists each estimated 30,000; Anglicans, 22,000; Presbyterians, 15,000; Quakers, 300; and Mormons, 50. The Mormons meet in Havana in space rented from another church. The Jewish community has 1,500 members; 1,200 reside in Havana. Most Protestant churches reported steady growth, including significant increases in the number of Pentecostals.

> According to the Islamic League, there are approximately 6,000 to 8,000 Muslims in the country, although only an estimated 1,000 are Cubans. The rest are temporarily resident foreigners,

---

[179] www.cia.gov/library/publications/the-world-factbook/docs/notesanddefs.html#2122

[180] US State Dept. http://1.usa.gov/VngJwI

mainly businessmen, students, and diplomats. In 2007 the government declined an offer by foreign donors to build a mosque in Havana, promising to undertake the project itself; however, construction had not begun by the end of the reporting period.

Interestingly, the State Department's report does not even mention Santería.

Recommended viewing—

Santeria—http://youtu.be/bNhA2IsT9R4

Afro-Cuban Santeria Ceremony—http://youtu.be/SSjEccnOvQQ

La Santeria en Matanzas, Cuba—http://youtu.be/2xq3yxf0HvY

Santeria Religious Ceremony—http://youtu.be/QuKro0rOmlg

Education

The most obvious feature of Cuban education is that it is free. For everyone. Through university, for those who are qualified.

Perhaps even more important is that not only is education held in high regard, but so are teachers. Because teachers are respected by parents, they are respected by students. The result is schools that succeed, populated by students and teachers who want to be in them.

Cuba's high regard for education was demonstrated just two years after the Revolution, when hundreds of thousands of Cubans, primarily youths, went throughout the country to teach illiterate Cubans how to read and write. The Cuban Literacy Campaign remains a remarkable example of what a country can accomplish—if its people have the will.

Free Universal Education

Education through university in Cuba is free for everyone

Primary School

There are nine primary school students to every teacher. (The US has fourteen.) [181] All children attend primary school from age 5 to 11 or 12.

Children at primary school have the same teacher for the first four years of their education, except in math and music. Curriculum also includes dance, gardening, and health and hygiene. All schools in Cuba have a doctor on site. Uniforms and meals are free. Mobile teachers are sent to the homes if children cannot come to school because of sickness or disability.

According to a report, "Cuban children excel academically for fairly straightforward reasons: they attend schools intensely focused on instruction, staffed by well-trained, regularly supervised teachers in a social environment that is dedicated to high achievement for all." [182]

---

[181] http://data.worldbank.org/indicator/SE.PRM.ENRL.TC.ZS

[182] Martin Carnoy, *Cuba's Academic Advantage*, http://bit.ly/R21ncG

Cuban schoolchildren
CREDIT: ADAM JONES ADAMJONES.FREESERVERS.COM

Bullying

Cuban schools have the lowest bullying rate in Latin America. More than 40 percent of students reported verbal or physical bullying in Colombia, Costa Rica, Argentina, Ecuador, Panama, Dominican Republic, Uruguay, Paraguay, Nicaragua, Brazil, Peru, Mexico, Guatemala, El Salvador and Chile. In Cuba the rate was just 13 percent. [183]

Secondary School

All children are required to remain in school through the age of 15. All students from age 12 to 15 go to basic secondary schools where academic standards are high and are exam-oriented. There are also vocational schools, where children age 12 and over can go to learn a trade. Vocational schools offer training as varied as carpentry, masonry, dance and renewable energy.

Young people wishing to continue their studies into higher education can do so at a high school, or a specialist school for advanced studies, military studies, sports or music.

Higher Education

Adult education at all levels is free, both onsite and via television. In 1959 there were only three universities. Today higher education is available in

---

[183] Economic Commission for Latin America   http://bit.ly/Vn91To

every one of the fifteen provinces with approximately forty-five universities and institutes, 24,800 professors, and a total enrollment of 250,000. [184]

The emphasis is on subjects which serve the needs of Cuba's development, such as teaching, medicine, science, engineering, and farm management. Students who graduate from an institution of higher education are guaranteed a job in their specialty.

The Cuban government spends more than twice as much of its budget as the US does on education. Cuba spends 12.9 percent of GDP (and 18.3 percent of all government spending) on education.[185] The US spends 5.4 percent. [186]

UNESCO's Education for All Global Monitoring Report 2012 praised Cuba's educational system

The report [187] says that Cuba "has achieved high standards of education quality, as measured by international tests" and that "the average performance level of its pupils was remarkably high compared to that of other countries in the region." It attributes this to:

- Education as a cornerstone of the Cuban Revolution
- Sustained investment
- Highly valued teachers
- Incentives to reward excellence of pupils, teachers and schools
- Principle of competition, solidarity and collaboration to encourage improvement
- Experience-sharing mechanisms for mutual learning and joint development of the curriculum

The report also notes that Cuba "emphasizes education's role in developing the whole individual (including physical education, sports, recreation and artistic education) while explicitly linking education with life, work and production," and "the high esteem in which the teaching profession is held in Cuba seems crucial to its success." [188]

---

[184] www.cubatreks.com/reports/vanthiel.php

[185] UNESCO http://bit.ly/YkWak8

[186] UNESCO http://bit.ly/VJTc4L

[187] www.unesco.org/en/efareport/reports/2005-quality/

[188] L. Gasperini (2000), *The Cuban Education System: Lessons and Dilemmas.* Washington, DC, World Bank. (World Bank Country Studies. Education Reform and Management Publication Series, Vol. 1, No. 5.)

Literacy

Cuba has one of the highest literacy rates in the world

Cuba's adult literacy rate (age 15 and older) is currently at 99.8 percent, as high as any other country. The same report shows the equivalent literacy rate in the United States as 98.2 percent. [189]

The Cuban people taught each other how to read and write

On September 26, 1960, Fidel Castro spoke to the United Nations General Assembly and vowed to eliminate illiteracy in Cuba by the end of the following year.

In 1961, more than 100,000 young people took part in the Cuban Literacy Campaign, as did another 50,000 adults and professional teachers. The average age of a volunteer was 15, with ages ranging from 10 to 19. Students came from elementary schools, high schools and universities. More than 60 percent were female. Over the entire year, an estimated 268,000 Cubans worked with the literacy campaign, and more than 707,000 Cubans became literate. Before the campaign, the country's literacy rate was 76 percent. By the end of the year, the campaign had raised the adult literacy rate (the ability to read and write at first grade level) from 76 percent to 96 percent.

---

[189] United Nations Develop Program Report 2011 -
http://hdr.undp.org/en/reports/global/hdr2011/

Parade of volunteer literacy teachers in
Havana at conclusion of Cuban Literacy Campaign.
CREDIT: ARCHIVAL

One goal of the Literacy Campaign was to teach urban youth about the life of the rural peasants

As Fidel Castro said,

> You will teach, and you will learn. You are going to learn much more than you can possibly teach...because while you teach them what you have learned in school, they will be teaching you what they have learned from the hard life that they have led. They will teach you the "why" of the revolution better than any speech, better than any book. [190]

And, as an educator said,

> The peasants discovered the word. The students discovered the poor. Together, they discovered their own homeland. [191]

Teachers lived and worked with their students, and taught them in the evening. This contact was designed to break through urban-rural barriers and the discrimination toward women and Cubans of African ancestry. More than 1.5 million primers were printed. They were designed around the

---

[190] Alexandra Keeble (ed.), *In the spirit of wandering teachers: Cuban Literacy Campaign 1961*, Melbourne: Ocean Press, 2001. p. 15

[191] Alexandra Keeble (ed.), *In the spirit of wandering teachers: Cuban Literacy Campaign 1961*, Melbourne: Ocean Press, 2001. p. 25

common vocabulary of Cuban farmers and expressed the political and social goals of the revolution.

> Thank you for giving me the opportunity to learn to read and write—now, nobody can deceive me and I can learn the truth for myself.
> —— A Cuban literacy student (from the book *In the Spirit of Wandering Teachers*)

Recommended viewing—

Maestra –a documentary film on the Cuban Literacy Campaign (see trailer) http://www.maestrathefilm.org/

Campaña de Alfabetización en Cuba (in Spanish) http://youtu.be/nbiN1-V9-Cw

Recommended reading—

In the Spirit of Wandering Teachers - Alexandra Keeble (ed), Ocean Press

Many volunteer teachers died during the Cuban Literacy Campaign

Not all of the volunteer literacy teachers survived. Some *campesinos* (peasants) were suspicious of the city youths, and groups of *banditos*—renegade Batista supporters, many backed by the United States—roamed the countryside. On January 5, 1961, just four days after the literacy campaign started, 18 year-old teacher Conrado Benítez was tortured and murdered by pro-Batista forces, as was the farmer he was teaching to read and write.

During the day Conrado had taught forty-four children, and at night another forty-four adults. When he was killed he had no weapon, only three books—on Anatomy, Mathematics and Composition—and some gifts for his students.

Conrado Benítez
Murdered literacy teacher.
CREDIT: ARCHIVAL

During the year-long campaign, fifteen volunteers were murdered (as were several of their students,) and another sixty-two died of illness or accident.

Chess

All students in Cuba have the opportunity to learn chess

Chess in Cuban schools was promoted by Che Guevara and has been an integral part of the Cuban school system since 1989. It is taught in almost all schools from first through ninth grades. Cuban universities now offer an undergraduate degree in chess.

It is taught in Cuban schools because the game of chess:

- Develops adaptability.
- Teaches ethics, as chess has rules that must be respected.
- Teaches how to make decisions independently and under pressure, which helps to strengthen character.
- Facilitates learning and to think before acting.
- Increases ability to concentrate.
- Increases levels of creativity and imagination.
- Develops patience and perseverance.
- Increases attention and self-esteem.
- Benefits the development of verbal and numerical cognitive skills.
- Develops logical reasoning, emotional intelligence and intuition.

Cuba for the Misinformed

- Exercises the ability to keep track of two or more parallel situations.
- Motivates study habits, reading and research in the field of philosophy, mathematics and computing.

Children playing chess on the street in Santiago de Cuba.
CREDIT: ADAM JONES ADAMJONES.FREESERVERS.COM

Health

If you saw the documentary film "Sicko," you already have some idea of the health care system in Cuba. If you did not and live in one of most developed countries, you will likely find Cuba's health system similar to your own. If you did not see the film and you live in the United States, you may have a problem identifying with the concept; particularly with the idea of free health care from a doctor in your neighborhood who even makes house calls.

One of the rights guaranteed in the Cuban Constitution is that "no sick person be left without medical care."

As a result, every Cuban is entitled to free health care. Cuba has a number of medical schools and produces a sufficient quantity of skilled medical practitioners that results in a ratio of physicians per capita that is extremely high. Cuba's life expectancy is one of the highest in the world and its healthcare system is recognized as a model for developing countries worldwide. Key to Cuba's success is its focus on preventative medicine. Its neighborhood doctors and nurses, working with public health officials, maintain continual contact with their neighbors to monitor health and health conditions. It pays off, keeping Cubans healthier and at lower cost.

Healthcare

Cuba provides free health care for every citizen

Prior to the 1959 revolution, 80 percent of the Cuban population had nothing like health insurance coverage. Life expectancy was low, and maternal and infant mortality rates were high.

The new government recognized that medicine alone could not improve the people's health condition, and that what was needed was a socio-economic transformation. So, in addition to increasing the number of health care professionals, the new government focused on dramatically changing such areas as housing, education and social security. The cornerstones of this change were equality of access, a holistic approach, and community participation.

Cuba provides free health care to all, including eye care, dental care and prescriptions. (The US currently has 40 million people without regular health care.) The Cuban focus is on *preventive* medical care in order to avoid the higher costs of treatment. House calls are routine and convenient because there is usually a doctor living in the neighborhood. This also enables medical workers to be aware of the family, home and neighborhood environment in which their patients live.

Cuba is a world leader in biotechnology, and has developed new vaccines and treatments for such diseases as malaria, hepatitis and dengue fever. The country has also turned more and more to alternative medicine. Physicians, including neighborhood doctors, are trained in the use of herbs and other natural remedies, and increasingly in the use of techniques such as acupuncture, aromatherapy, yoga, tai chi, and other non-pharmaceutical procedures.

Because there is a national health care system, the government is able to monitor the health conditions of all its people. Potential epidemics of diseases, such as malaria or dengue fever, can be spotted quickly and eradicated through a nationwide effort. As a result, Cubans no longer experience diphtheria, polio, or measles, have the lowest AIDS rate in the Americas, and have the highest rate of treatment for, and control of, hypertension.

Patients also have access to treatment beyond the skills and abilities of their neighborhood physicians. Nearby *policlinicos* ("polyclinics"—specialty clinics) provide specialists, laboratories, rehabilitation and physical therapy. Cuba provides all of these additional medical services free of charge to all Cubans. There are currently 281 hospitals and 442 polyclinics in the country, as well as other specialized centers.

Cuba has one of the highest life expectancies in the world

The current life expectancy is 79.1 years. The US is 78.5 years. [192]

Cuba spends just $204 per person per year on health care

Even with the high levels of health care access, every Cuban is insured at no charge. The US government spends $2,368 per person, more than any other country in the world, [193] yet 40 million Americans are uninsured. (Countries such as Germany, France, Canada and Switzerland spend less per capita, yet every one of their citizens is insured.) Total expenditure per capita, including both government and private payments, is $6,096 in the US, higher than any other country. In Cuba, the per capita total of both patient and government costs is $229. [194]

---

[192] http://hdrstats.undp.org/en/indicators/69206.html

[193] http://data.worldbank.org/indicator/SH.XPD.PCAP

[194] NationMaster http://bit.ly/X9T17F

Cuba has proportionally more hospital beds than the US

Cuba has 49 hospital beds per 10,000 population compared to 32 for the US. [195]

Cuba has the second highest number of physicians per thousand people in the world

Cuba has 5.91 physicians—including neighborhood, specialists and researchers—per thousand people. (San Marino is off in its own medical world with 47.35. The US comes in at fifty-second place with 2.3)

Cuba focuses on primary health care

Eighty percent of Cuba's physicians are primary care doctors with only 20 percent trained as specialists. In the US these percentages are reversed. [196] This focus on primary care reflects the Cuban health system's emphasis on preventive measures rather than on dealing with more advanced—and more costly—medical problems.

A typical primary doctor is responsible for 1,000 patients— all of them neighbors

Doctors operate out of local neighborhood clinics with the help of a nurse, a social worker, and a statistician. If a patient needs more care than the clinic can provide, the patient is sent to the local *policlinico*, which has specialty physicians. [197]

When neighbors do not like their neighborhood doctor, they may choose a different one.

Cuba has one of the lowest HIV infection rates in the world

Cuba's infection rate is 0.1 percent, similar to that of Finland and Singapore. This is one-sixth of the rate in the US, and one-twentieth of the rate of Cuba's neighbor Haiti, which has been devastated by HIV/AIDS. [198]

Cuba was one of the first countries that needed to confront HIV/AIDS because many of the doctors, soldiers, engineers, teachers and others that it had sent to Africa in the 1960s and 1970s began returning home with the

---

[195] http://apps.who.int/whosis/data/Search.jsp

[196] www.healthcareitnews.com/news/mgma-delegation-cuba-discovers-lot-about-healthcare

[197] www.healthcareitnews.com/news/mgma-delegation-cuba-discovers-lot-about-healthcare

[198] New York Times   http://nyti.ms/REd2fM

disease. As a result, Cuba was also one of the first countries to take aggressive action against the epidemic.

Cuba has an extremely effective system for dealing with all types of sexually-transmitted diseases. [199]

- Free universal health care. Out of a population of 11 million, Cuba has 535,000 health care workers.
- Large-scale distribution of free condoms (more than 100 million a year) with a focus on high-risk groups such as prostitutes and in places (such as pizzerias) where young people are customers. As a result, the HIV rate is much higher among homosexual/bisexual men than it is among prostitutes, and very low for young, unmarried women.
- Safe-sex education programs at all levels of school.
- High rates of HIV testing.
- Tracking sexual contacts of those who test positive, who must also take a two-week course on living responsibly with HIV.
- Pregnant women receive up to twelve free prenatal checkups, during which they are tested for HIV at least twice.

Fidel Castro received a gold medal from the World Health Organization

The text of the presentation reads:

> 1998 Award of the World Health Organization Health-for-All Gold Medal to His Excellency Dr Fidel Castro, President of the Republic of Cuba.
>
> It is in recognition of this leadership, and this continuing commitment to the social goal of health for all, that the World Health Organization is privileged to present the Health-for-All Gold Medal to His Excellency Dr Fidel Castro, President of the Republic of Cuba.
>
> But it is at the national and district levels that the President has devoted the bulk of his efforts for health, which he has rightly perceived as critically important for overall sustainable development. The country's national health system, with its emphasis on primary health care managed by a "health team," is widely considered to be exemplary.

---

[199] New York Times http://nyti.ms/REd2fM

Alternative Medicine

Sixty percent of Cubans use traditional or complementary / alternative medicine.

Sixty percent of allopathic (Western pharmaceutical-based) physicians are also trained in traditional and complementary/alternative forms of medicine. These forms of healing include both traditional Cuban healing methods (such as those used in Santería) as well as many other non-allopathic methods. [200] In addition, Cuba produces 579 registered herbal products and currently imports another 295.

Acupuncture (a traditional Chinese system working with the energy channels of the body) and homeopathy (a system for the treatment of disease by minute doses of natural substances that in a healthy person would produce symptoms of disease) were officially recognized in 1992, and homeopathic dispensaries are located throughout Cuba. All medical and pharmaceutical schools have introductory and advanced homeopathy courses. In 1995, a traditional medicine program was instituted, prioritizing the cultivation of medicinal plants, the education of practitioners, research into traditional medicine, and the integration of traditional medicine into the national health care system. [201]

---

[200] http://mediccreview.medicc.org/articles/mr_50.pdf

[201] World Health Organization http://bit.ly/UskBHd

Economy

The most important thing that can be said about the economy of Cuba is that it has survived. It has survived more than fifty years of an attack by the planet's largest economic and military power just ninety miles away.

Cuba's three main income sources are nickel, sugar, and tourism. Cuba has the fourth-largest nickel reserves in the world, its nickel production being in partnership with a Canadian corporation. The world market price of nickel has been high for some years, and this has been a great help to Cuba.

Cuba's sugar market was destroyed when US President Dwight Eisenhower unilaterally canceled that country's contract for Cuban sugar. For many years afterwards Cuba benefitted by the sale of its sugar to the Soviet Union at a highly-inflated price. After the Soviet Union fell, ending its financial assistance to Cuba in many other areas as well as sugar, Cuba's economy went into a tailspin—Cuba's "Special Period." Sugar is just starting to rise again as a viable export product.

Tourism was a primary income prior to the Revolution. American tourists could hop a plane or ferry, be there in a short time, and enjoy the delights of Cuba. This tourism also included Mafia-controlled casinos, and prostitution. The Revolution ended this form of tourism.

But it was not the end of tourism. Many tourists visit Cuba every year, but most are not from the US. You can read more about that in our "Tourism" section. It is sufficient to recognize that tourism remains an important part of the Cuban economy.

Cuba's main economic resources are tourism, nickel and sugar

Tourism brings more than two million visitors a year. Sugar has had a resurgence since the demand for the production of ethanol. Cuba has the world's second largest nickel deposits (after Russia.) Other exports include tobacco, coffee, rum, citrus fruit, pharmaceuticals, and biotechnology.

The US is a one-way trading partner with Cuba

The US sells some products (primarily agricultural) *to* Cuba but refuses to purchase goods *from* Cuba.

Cuban imports come from: Venezuela 35.2 percent, China 11.7 percent, Spain 8.5 percent, Brazil 4.6 percent, Canada 4.2 percent, United States 4.1 percent (2010) [202]

Cuban exports go to: China 25.5 percent, Canada 23.3 percent, Venezuela 10 percent, Spain 5.6 percent (2010) [203]

The average pay in Cuba is $21 a month

In 2011 the average monthly salary was 460 pesos, which is equivalent to US $21.03.[204] Food is heavily subsidized by the government, so that for 80 cents (US), a Cuban can buy 10 eggs, 7 pounds of rice, 2.2 pounds of chicken, 10 ounces of beans and 8 ounces of soy meal.[205]

When considering this average pay, it is important to remember that the government provides free health care and education as well as housing and subsidized food.

The majority of Cubans own their own homes

Electricity averages 5-7 pesos (20-28 cents) a month, gas is 2-4 pesos (8-16 cents), telephone 6-8 pesos (24-32 cents). [206] Although everyone is housed, the majority are housed poorly in small, crowded and deteriorating homes. The government has lacked funds to restore and build housing, the American blockade has prevented access to Cuba's cheapest and most convenient source of building materials, and the block housing provided (and unfortunately designed) with the help of the Soviet Union is coldly institutional and very un-Cuban.

Biotechnology

Cuba is a world leader in biotechnology

Biotechnology in Cuba started in 1965 when the country opened the first of its biotechnology research centers. In 1981 Cuba experienced an epidemic of dengue fever, which many believe was a result of US bioterrorism. Cuba responded by producing interferon to deal with the epidemic. In 1986 Cuba created its Center for Genetic Engineering and Biotechnology and its biotech

---

[202] https://www.cia.gov/library/publications/the-world-factbook/geos/cu.html

[203] https://www.cia.gov/library/publications/the-world-factbook/geos/cu.html

[204] www.state.gov/r/pa/ei/bgn/2886.htm

[205] Bloomberg http://bloom.bg/So1TRw

[206] www.drakecentral.info/cuba/Economy/pesos.htm

products have been recognized worldwide. Its products are exported to countries all over the world—except to the United States, which bans the importation of products from Cuba.

The US ban means that Americans are unable to have access to such medicines as vaccines against meningitis B and C and Hepatitis B; treatments for the eye disease *retinitis pigmentosa*; PPG—a cholesterol-reducing drug with a side effect of increasing sexual potency; and a therapeutic vaccine for lung cancer that extends life and can ease breathing and restore appetite. [207]

Cuba does not develop biological weapons

The US Government has at times accused—or at least implied—that Cuba was doing research into biological warfare, but has never offered a shred of proof. Former president Jimmy Carter visited Cuba in 2002. Before his trip, he queried US government authorities—including the White House, the CIA and the State Department—asking if Cuba was supporting any terrorist activities, including biological weapons. *All* replied that Cuba was not. [208]

Cigars

US President John F. Kennedy (reluctantly) banned Cuban cigars

A month after the Bay of Pigs fiasco, President Kennedy called Press Secretary Pierre Salinger into his room late in the afternoon, and said he needed 1,000 Cuban Petit Upmann cigars by the following morning.

The next morning at 8 a.m., Salinger came into the Oval Office and the president asked how he had done. Salinger replied that he had found 1,200 of the cigars. Kennedy said "Fantastic," opened up his desk door, pulled out the decree banning all Cuban products from the United States, and signed it. [209]

---

[207] http://margotpepper.com/node/42

[208] www.cartercenter.org/news/documents/doc623.html

[209] http://youtu.be/dHazLBTZUEs

John Kennedy liked but banned Cuban cigars
CREDIT: ARCHIVAL

Years later, in a *New York Times* article, former presidential assistant Richard Goodwin mentioned that Kennedy had told him he had not intended to include Cuban cigars in the embargo, but that lobbying by cigar manufacturers in Tampa forced him to include them as well. [210]

Recommended viewing—

Salinger's JFK-Cuban cigar stories—http://youtu.be/dHazLBTZUEs

---

[210] http://www.nytimes.com/2000/07/05/opinion/president-kennedy-s-plan-for-peace-with-cuba.html

It is illegal for an American to smoke a Cuban cigar in Mexico (or anywhere else)

If you are a permanent resident of the United States, or an American citizen living anywhere in the world, you are not allowed to smoke a Cuban cigar or enjoy a drink made with Cuban rum. Not in Mexico. Not in Canada. Not anywhere.

From the Office of Foreign Assets Control (OFAC), US Department of the Treasury:

> Transactions Involving Cuban-Origin Goods in Third Countries
>
> The question is often asked whether US citizens or permanent resident aliens of the United States may legally purchase Cuban origin goods, including tobacco and alcohol products, in a third country for personal use outside the United States. The answer is no. The Regulations prohibit persons subject to the jurisdiction of the United States from purchasing, transporting, importing, or otherwise dealing in or engaging in any transactions with respect to any merchandise outside the United States if such merchandise (1) is of Cuban origin; or (2) is or has been located in or transported from or through Cuba; or (3) is made or derived in whole or in part of any article which is the growth, produce or manufacture of Cuba. Thus, in the case of cigars, the prohibition extends to cigars manufactured in Cuba and sold in a third country and to cigars manufactured in a third country from tobacco grown in Cuba. [211]

Criminal penalties for violation of the regulations range up to $1,000,000 in fines for corporations, or $250,000 and up to ten years in prison for individuals. Civil penalties of up to $65,000 per violation may be imposed by OFAC.

The US sanctions against Cuba apply to more people than you might think

According to OFAC, these sanctions regulations apply to "all US citizens and permanent residents wherever they are located, all people and organizations physically in the United States, and all branches and subsidiaries of US organizations throughout the world." [212]

---

[211] www.treasury.gov/resource-center/sanctions/Documents/ccigar2.pdf

[212] www.treasury.gov/resource-center/sanctions/programs/pages/cuba.aspx

Most professional cigar rollers in Cuba are women

Although before the revolution most cigar rollers were men (*torcedores*), today the majority are women (*torcedoras*.) [213] A roller can make from 60 to 150 cigars a day, depending on the shape of the cigar. [214]

Many cigar rollers listen to someone reading aloud while they work

Historically the rollers have listened to someone reading from newspapers and popular novels (selected by a vote of the rollers). Before the revolution, cigar rollers were considered the most educated workers in Cuba because of the readers and the passionate discussions on rest breaks about what they had just heard. Cigar brands such as *Montecristo* and *Romeo y Julieta* were allegedly named after books or plays that the workers had listened to. [215]

There are still an estimated 250 readers (*lectores*) at cigar factories in Cuba. [216]

Cuban cigars are not rolled on the thighs of virgins

In fact they are not rolled on the thighs of anyone. One simply needs to attempt to roll a cigar that way in order to discover that it just will not work. [217]

Fidel Castro does not smoke cigars

He used to, starting at the age of 15, but he stopped at the age of 59 for health reasons. His favorite cigar was the *Cohiba Esplendido.*

Recommended viewing—

Cuban Cigars – The complete process—http://youtu.be/ynJlJn0WFZc

---

[213] www.habanos.com/article.aspx?aid=24

[214] http://en.cigar-wiki.com/Torcedores

[215] www.cigaraficionado.com/webfeatures/show/id/Rolling-by-the-Book_3155/p/1

[216] http://news.bbc.co.uk/2/hi/8406641.stm

[217] www.smokemag.com/0604/feature.htm

Currency

Tourists use different money than Cubans

Cubans buy staples and food with Cuban Pesos; tourists use Convertible Pesos (CUC) which can be used in foreign exchange. In Varadero and other prime tourist locations, tourists can also pay in euros. Credit cards are accepted unless they are from US banks. Travelers checks, including those from US banks, are accepted. [218]

Cuban currency (CUP) for use by Cubans. Portrait is of Camilo Cienfuegos.
CREDIT: CENTRAL BANK OF CUBA

Special Period

Cuba's Special Period was a prototype for the world of diminished resources

Cuba has already been through economic collapse as a result of the shortage of energy resources, and there may be much we can learn from that country. Their own "Peak Oil" happened after the Soviet Union collapsed in 1989 and Cuba lost its primary sugar market along with the source of most of its petroleum and other fossil fuels and raw materials.

The Cubans rose to the occasion, and today Cuba is a model of sustainability for the rest of the world. But it required much sacrifice. Cuba euphemistically refers to this difficult time as its "Special Period (*Período especial*) in time of peace."

Prior to the collapse of the USSR, Cuba received huge support from the Soviet Bloc countries. Cuban sugar was purchased at five times the world

---

[218] www.dtcuba.com/CubaInfo.aspx?lng=2#Inicio

price, and the Soviet countries provided Cuba with 98 percent of its petroleum. Cuba received so much petroleum that it was able to re-sell some of that oil on the world market in order to gain hard currency.

As a result of this greatly-subsidized fossil fuel supply, Cuba became heavily dependent on gasoline and natural gas for transportation and agriculture. It used tractors—more than 20,000 of them—on its large, industrial, state-owned farms (one agronomist said that Cuba had more tractors per acre than California had.) Like the US, Cuba treated its crops with heavy applications of pesticides, insecticides, and herbicides.

The country exported trade crops such as tobacco, sugar, coffee and citrus fruits and imported 66 percent of its basic staples. It also imported 86 percent of all raw materials, and 80 percent of machinery and spare parts, most of this from Soviet Bloc countries.

When trade with the USSR disappeared, Cuba lost 53 percent of its petroleum imports and 85 percent of its trade economy. The country also lost 77 percent of its imported fertilizer, that amount dropping from 1.3 million tons per year to 300,000 tons. Its imports of animal feed dropped 70 percent, and its pesticide imports in terms of dollar value fell 63 percent.

Cuba recognized that for its own survival it would have to interact with the capitalist world market, including legalizing the use of US dollars, accepting foreign investment, allowing at least limited self-employment, and welcoming tourism. During this period, as it does today, the severe economic embargo by the US remained in effect.

Cuba also realized that because of the economic crisis it could not at the time continue expanding its efforts towards a socialist society. However, it was still committed to maintaining what it had already achieved in the areas of health care, education, employment, culture, defense and solidarity with other countries worldwide.

Cuba also vowed that there would be none of the privatization, mass firings, and drastic cuts in social spending that were being demanded of other Latin American countries by the World Bank and the International Monetary Fund. Cuban workers whose factories were stilled because of lack of raw materials or energy did not lose their jobs but went home while continuing to receive 60 percent of their salary. No schools, hospitals, homes for the elderly or child care centers were closed. No one became homeless.

Prior to the Soviet collapse, food imports constituted 66 percent of the food consumed by Cubans. Those imports dropped by 50 percent. The country's own food production dropped by 45 percent. The daily per capita caloric intake decreased 36 percent, protein intake dropped 40 percent, and the consumption of dietary fats fell 65 percent. Most Cuban adults lost an average of 20-30 pounds in weight.

Thanks to strong government programs, the results of food shortages were not as bad as they could have been. Children, the elderly, and pregnant and lactating mothers were ensured healthy levels of caloric intake, and a ration card system guaranteed everyone a basic, minimum level of food. In 1995-7, the average daily intake was 1863 calories and 55 grams of protein, considerably below the World Health Organizations' recommended 2400 calories and 72 grams of protein; today it has returned to an average of more than 3420 calories and 80 grams of proteins.

Recommended viewing—

The Power of Community: How Cuba survived Peak Oil
http://youtu.be/L2TzvnRo6_c

How Cuba survived Peak Oil—http://youtu.be/yIC-0JYoDs8

Sugar

The US canceled its sugar purchase agreement with Cuba in 1959, forcing Cuba to rely on the Soviet Union

Cuba had been a major supplier of sugar to the United States, but in July 1959, the US canceled Cuba's sugar quota and refused to honor its commitment to buy the 700,000 tons remaining from the 1960 quota. It was the first move of the US blockade of Cuba and ultimately forced Cuba to turn to the Soviet Union for economic support.

Cuba for the Misinformed

Che Guevara cutting sugar cane
CREDIT: ARCHIVAL

Recommended viewing—

Cuba – Loading the cane and hauling it to the mill
http://youtu.be/pSreXQ1Kc2A
Inside a Cuban steam powered sugar mill—http://youtu.be/Z_UP6TyQ5eI

Sustainability

Cuba's Special Period, when it could no longer afford to import insecticides, pesticides, and fertilizers for its crops, led Cubans to focus on organic agricultural production. Agronomists and some farmers had advocated growing organically for years; it took a crisis and lack of chemicals to make that happen. But now Cuba is fully committed to sustainability—a commitment that can be seen in the extensive network of organic gardens within Cuban cities.

Cuba's focus is not just on food. Reforestation, energy-saving measures, and environmental-awareness are all examples of the country's determination to make sustainability a way of life.

In 2006 the World Wildlife Foundation declared Cuba to be the only country in the world that was approaching sustainable development

Most countries talk green. According to the World Wildlife Foundation only one lives it. In 2006 the foundation declared Cuba to be the only country in the world that was approaching sustainable development. The study's authors credited Cuba's "high level of literacy, long life expectancy and low consumption of energy" for its success in sustainability.

Only Cuba passed in two areas of measurement:

- The United Nations' Human Development Index, which is calculated from life expectancy, literacy and education, and per capita Gross Domestic Product;
- The "ecological footprint", which shows the energy and resources consumed per person in each country.

Sustainable development was defined by the foundation as "a commitment to improving the quality of human life while living within the carrying capacity of supporting ecosystems."

Agriculture

Cuba is a world leader in community and urban gardens

An Organopónico (urban garden) in Havana.

The Cuban government and its people have created community gardens in cities and towns throughout Cuba. Actually, the people started it first; the government then got on the bandwagon and supported them. The larger state-supported and cooperative organic farms are called *organopónicos;* smaller neighborhood and patio gardens are *huertos.* The outskirts of cities provide still more space for gardens, and there are even gardens attached to factories and office buildings, where the workers are able to produce food for lunchtime meals and to take home. All of these types and sizes of gardens increase the country's food production, and avoid the need for fuel to transport food from the countryside into the cities.

Havana has a population of a little over 2 million people, and its gardens currently produce more than 4,000,000 tons of food annually,[219] amounting to 90 percent of the fruits and vegetables its residents consume. [220] Community gardens produce, by law, only organic food. Most goes to the people who work in the gardens. Surplus is donated to schools, senior centers and other community programs, and is often sold in farmers markets.

The country's urban agriculture program, begun in 1988, has created jobs for 354,000 people out of a national workforce of five million. [221]

---

[219] CivilEats.com http://bit.ly/Usawdl

[220] Rodale Institute http://bit.ly/SnZUMX

[221] CivilEats.com http://bit.ly/Usawdl

Cuba is one of the most organically-farmed countries in the world.

Prior to the Special Period (when the collapse of the Soviet Union meant the loss of most of Cuba's oil and fertilizer imports) there were already a number of scientists and agricultural experts who had been urging the country to move toward more organic and sustainable methods of farming in order to combat soil erosion and mineral depletion. When oil imports collapsed, these experts moved into action. The result is perhaps the most organically oriented and self-sustaining country in the world. However, some crops, such as rice and tobacco, continue to require chemical-based fertilizers and pesticides.

Cuba today uses oxen instead of tractors wherever possible. "Animal traction" saves fuel, avoids soil compaction and turns the soil to a healthier level. In just a few years after Soviet oil subsidies disappeared, the number of teams of oxen in the country increased from 50,000 to 400,000. As side benefits, there was a new cottage industry in harness shops, and the number of blacksmiths quadrupled.

Cuba was formerly dependent on petroleum-based pesticides and natural gas-based fertilizers. Today the country mainly uses "biofertilizers" such as manure, compost, vermiculture (earthworms), nitrogen-rich cover crops (green manure) and crop rotation; and "biopesticides" such as microbes, natural biological predators, resistant varieties of plants, and complementary crops.

Cuba today uses less than five percent of the amount of pesticides that it used before 1989 (1,000 tons compared to 21,000 tons). The Cubans have decreased, by necessity, the amount of meat in their diet and increased the amount of fruits and vegetables. The health of the people—for example, a 25 percent decline in heart disease—and the government coffers benefit greatly from the decreased use of pesticides and the increased healthy diet.

Recommended viewing—

Organopónico – An Agricultural Revolution—http://youtu.be/JIWsxo5nNgg

Cuba – The Accidental Revolution (short clip)
http://youtu.be/JzbmxZBTbt4

Energy

Cubans per capita use 5-6 percent of the energy consumed by residents of the US

To conserve fossil fuels and to generate energy close to the actual users of the energy, Cuba has moved toward small-scale renewable energy production. It has begun using photovoltaic panels to generate solar energy throughout the country. Solar power currently provides energy to more than 2,000 schools and hundreds of hospitals. In a recent energy program the government distributed more than 9 million free compact fluorescent light bulbs to Cuban households. It also distributed 3.5 million electric rice cookers, 2.5 million electric cook pots, 2.3 million water heaters, and 250,000 energy-efficient refrigerators, all of which will use much less energy than the appliances they replaced. All of these utensils were Chinese-made, and sold by the Cuban government at heavily-subsidized prices with monthly payments.

"Cuba needs to save electricity"
CREDIT: MARSHALL SOULES

Las Terrazas

Cuba has created a beautiful community for "nature tourism" in a previously deforested area

Las Terrazas (The Terraces) is a community in a mountainous area designated a Biosphere Reserve by UNESCO. [222] It is located in Pinar del Rio province, to the west of Havana. The location had previously been cleared for coffee and cattle, but the forest has now been restored with 8 million trees planted over an area of 5,000 hectares between 1983 and 1990.[223] Today the small community offers hotels, restaurants, crafts, locally-produced coffee, and hiking through beautiful forests. [224]

Las Terrazas community, Pinar del Rio Province

Recommended viewing—

Las Terrazas—http://youtu.be/53S8Pc7Y3Aw

---

[222] www.dtcuba.com/showreport.aspx?lng=2&c=48

[223] www.guardian.co.uk/travel/2009/dec/12/cubas-green-revolution

[224] www.cuba-lasterrazas.com/

Sports

When Americans think of Cuban sports, they think of baseball. No surprise, since so many outstanding US baseball players have come from Cuba. Baseball is the national sport of Cuba, but their record in the Olympic Games shows Cuba has gold-winning skills in many other sports. It is clear, however, that golf will not be one of them for some time.

Baseball

Cubans have been playing baseball since the 1860s

Baseball was introduced to Cuba by Cubans who had studied in the US and by American sailors on shore leave in Havana and other Cuban ports.

There are no professional sports in Cuba. The Cuban National Baseball Team is composed of amateur players from the national leagues. The team competed in every summer Olympics from 1992 to 2008 (baseball was voted out of the Olympics starting in 2012) and for those years was the most successful team in those games. Out of five Olympiads, they won gold three times and silver twice. The Cuban national baseball team reached the finals of the 2006 (and first) World Baseball Classic, losing to tournament winner Japan 10-6.

Logo of Los Industriales
CREDIT: LOS INDUSTRIALES

The Los Industriales are Havana's (and Cuba's) equivalent of the New York Yankees.

Recommended viewing—

Baseball in Havana— http://youtu.be/YFJ0rx2UeTg

Cuba allowed black baseball players 47 years before the US

Cuban teams opened to black players in 1900, and many players from the US Negro League moved to Cuba to play for those teams. It wasn't until 1947 that the US major leagues allowed black players, Jackie Robinson being the very first.

Fidel Castro and Camilo Cienfuegos play exhibition baseball.
CREDIT: ARCHIVAL

Fidel Castro never played baseball on any team in Cuba, and did not miss a chance to be recruited for a major American team

These are common but false rumors often heard in the United States. The only direct connection between Fidel Castro and baseball is that soon after Castro and his guerrilla army came to power, Castro pledged to underwrite the debts of the Havana Sugar Kings baseball team with an exhibition contest between his own pickup squad *Los Barbudos* ("The Bearded Ones") and a military police team. Castro reportedly pitched one inning, earning two strikeouts, although some say the umpire might have been biased in Castro's favor.

Havana has a special place for fans to argue about baseball

The best place in Cuba to discuss baseball is *la esquina caliente*, or "the hot corner"—baseball jargon for third base—located in Parque Central (Central Park) just across the street from the capitol building. Dozens of men gather there daily to talk, and argue, about baseball.

Talking baseball at *La Esquina Caliente* (The Hot Corner)
CREDIT: IAN USHER/FLICKR[225]

Recommended viewing—

La Esquina Caliente—http://youtu.be/vU58IgP21bw

Olympics

Cuba has won seventy-two Olympic gold medals

Cuba has participated in the Summer Olympic Games since 1900 and has competed in nineteen of the twenty-six Games. Cuba has won seventy-two gold medals, with its major award-winning sports being boxing, track and field, wrestling, judo, fencing, baseball, volleyball and weightlifting.

Golf

There is only one 18-hole golf course in the entire country of Cuba

Cuba is not (yet) a golfer's paradise. The only 18-hole golf course in the country is *Varadero Golf Club*[226] in Cuba's most popular resort area. The only other golf course in the country (except for the American course at

---

[225] http://flic.kr/p/6hHnYy

[226] www.varaderogolfclub.com

Guantánamo) is the nine-hole Havana Golf Club just ten minutes from the center of Havana. The Cuban government has made arrangements with international developers to construct other courses in the country. [227]

Varadero Golf Club.
CREDIT: VARADERO GOLF CLUB

When Cuba's revolutionary government took over, golf was considered to be a rich man's sport symbolic of the Batista government, so it was not high on the new government's list of priorities.

As one American business consultant has said:

> The conflict is imagery versus profit. Concerns about the image of golfers in the worker's paradise. And, if accepted, how does *Granma* (the Communist Party newspaper) explain the obese US golfer with poor clothing colour co-ordination, running about in their "Caddyshack" like golf cart, betting on each hole? [228]

---

[227] www.havanatimes.org/?p=53036

[228] http://usatoday30.usatoday.com/travel/destinations/2010-04-26-cuba-golf_N.htm

It might have helped if Castro and his colleagues had been golfers, but if a game of golf that Fidel Castro and Che Guevara played a month before the Bay of Pigs invasion is any indication, golf was not one of their strengths.

Che Guevara and Fidel Castro play golf
CREDIT: ALBERTO KORDA

According to reports, on a par-70 course, Che shot a 127 and Fidel finished the round with a 150. [229]

Recommended viewing—

Varadero Golf Club—http://youtu.be/vCEKyfDYxAY

---

[229] MSN Travel http://on-msn.com/U7zFzx

Havana

Havana is the capital city of Cuba, and the former Capital of the Americas during the days of the Spanish Empire. It is the Cuban city most often visited by tourists and, as those tourists well know, one of the most photogenic cities in the world. Habana Vieja (Old Havana) is the best-known area of the city, but there is much more to be seen. When you visit Havana, try to see at least a few of the city's fourteen other districts.

Capital City of the Americas

Havana was the Spanish Empire's Capital City of the Americas

Havana (*La Habana*) is a remarkable city. It is at once majestic and decrepit, vital and decaying. It was founded in the sixteenth century and at one time was the Spanish Empire's shining jewel of the New World; the capital of all of Spain's enterprises throughout the Americas. Loot from the entire region was brought to Havana before being shipped to Spain to be divided up between the Royal Treasury and commercial backers of the expeditions and colonies. By the mid-1800s, Havana, with a population of more than 30,000, was the third largest city in the Americas, smaller than Lima and Mexico City but larger than Boston or New York. [230] Today it has a population of 2.1 million.

---

[230] Hugh Thomas, *Cuba or the Pursuit of Freedom*, Da Capo Press (1998)

Cuba for the Misinformed

Habana Vieja (Old Havana)
CREDIT: KAMIRA/BIGSTOCK

Plaza Vieja (Old Plaza)
CREDIT: ALEKSANDAR TODOROVIC/BIGSTOCK

Cuba's original Capitol Building (El Capitolio) was modeled somewhat after the US Capitol. It was completed in 1929 and served as the seat of government until 1959.

El Capitolio
CREDIT: DZAIN/BIGSTOCK

Recommended Viewing—

La Habana Vieja—http://youtu.be/MNrOPpJXdFs

Habana Vieja (Old Havana) tour—http://youtu.be/gmE0J7F2G8s

My City, La Habana—http://youtu.be/IdwP6zeT0DA

Cuban Son in Habana Vieja—http://youtu.be/TPnD4-RNprl

Central Havana Tour (in four parts)
http://www.cuba-junky.com/havana/todo_havana_centro.htm

Havana Club City Guide—http://youtu.be/yjpoIY02XwA

John Lennon

There is a park in Havana named after John Lennon

In the Vedado district of Havana, where the University of Havana is located, is a small public park named the "John Lennon Park." It is a favorite spot for tourists because in the park is a bench upon which sits a sculpture of Beatle John Lennon by José Villa Soberón. Inscribed in the cement in front of the bench are the lyrics in Spanish from Lennon's song "Imagine"

John Lennon and friend in John Lennon Park, Havana

*Dirar que soy un soñador
pero no soy el unico*

*(You may say that I'm a dreamer
but I'm not the only one)*

Ice Cream

Havana's favorite ice cream parlor starred in an award-winning film

Coppelia is an ice cream parlor in the Vedado district of Havana. It serves more than 25,000 people daily, and was the setting for the award-winning Cuban film "Strawberry and Chocolate." Coppelia has two outlets where the ice cream is served. One is for customers paying with Cuban pesos, and another—with much shorter lines—for those paying with the more expensive Convertible Pesos, used by foreigners. Caution: Cubans say the ice cream isn't what it used to be.

Cubans waiting in queue for Coppelia ice cream, Havana.

Recommended viewing—

Coppelia Ice Cream Parlour—http://youtu.be/V9lN3qeeulU

Malecón

Havana's best known street is right on the ocean—and faces north towards the US

The Malecón (officially *Avenida de Maceo*) is a broad esplanade—a roadway and seawall which stretches for eight kilometers (about 5 miles) along the coast from the mouth of Havana Harbor in Old Havana, along the north side of the Centro Habana neighborhood, and ends in the Vedado neighborhood. Construction of the Malecón began in 1901, when the US military controlled the country.

Cuba for the Misinformed

The Malecón, Havana
CREDIT: LUKAS MATHIS/WIKIMEDIA COMMONS

Malecón
CREDIT:SPANISHALEX/BIGSTOCK

View of Morro Castle from the Malecón
CREDIT: MARSHALL SOULES

El Paseo del Prado where people can stroll all the way
from the Malecón to El Capitolio and Parque Central
CREDIT: KAMIRA/BIGSTOCK

Recommended viewing—

Drive along the Malecón—http://youtu.be/2CnqIFjxc40

Malecón Drive—http://youtu.be/WvE26Gbgd8Y

Sea Boulevard Malecón—http://youtu.be/56-8dyHEXyY

University of Havana

The University of Havana was founded in 1728

La Universidad de la Habana is one of the oldest universities in the Americas, founded by the Dominicans in 1728. Today it has more than 6,000 students with sixteen faculties (colleges) in Havana.

University of Havana, Havana, Cuba.
CREDIT: TAKETHEMUD/WIKIMEDIA COMMONS

There are also twenty-two other universities throughout Cuba.

Recommended viewing—

University of Havana Tour—http://youtu.be/YVlO8vuxJjU

Urban Planning

The architecture and buildings of Havana are not what they used to be—but they're still beautiful

At its zenith Havana was an architectural jewel, supported by the wealth of the entire Americas, from the gold and silver mines of Mexico to the tin mines of Bolivia and the plantations of Central America and the Caribbean. But that was hundreds of years ago, and the Spanish Empire that created and sustained Havana is long gone.

La Maqueta - scale model of city of Havana.

Is it possible to maintain such a city and its complex infrastructure without the resources of an empire? The Cubans are doing the best that they can under difficult conditions, conditions not helped by the active resistance of the world's superpower just ninety miles away. It may be, however, that it would be impossible today for even a wealthy country to restore all of the magnificent buildings of Havana to their original state.

Nevertheless, improving housing and restoring historic buildings (particularly to help generate badly-needed tourist income) is a high priority for the national and municipal governments. Havana's Office of the Architect is tasked with restoring and maintaining Havana's historic buildings, particularly those in *La Habana Vieja* (Old Havana). Visitors to Havana can see the results of these efforts, and the buildings and historic plazas are magnificent.

The restoration efforts are greatly hindered by the US blockade of Cuba which requires Cuba to import building materials at much greater cost than if it were to purchase materials and equipment from only ninety miles away.

Havana has the second largest urban planning model in the world

Havana's city planners, the Group for the Integral Development of the Capitol, have created a 1:1000 scale model (La Maqueta) of the entire city of Havana that is the second largest in the world (New York City has the largest, but it is no longer used for urban planning purposes.) The model is currently 22 meters long, and 10 meters wide to represent Havana's 727 square kilometers. It took nine years to build, much of it from cigar boxes.

Colors are used to indicate a building's historical period of construction. Brown indicates the Spanish colonial period, ochre represents the republican period, ivory the revolutionary period since 1959, and white represents new projects, as well as monuments and cemeteries. Vegetation, parks, beaches and other areas are all textured and appropriately colored.

Cuba for the Misinformed

With this model, representations of proposed buildings can be placed within the miniature city, and it can be seen exactly how the building will relate to surrounding buildings—often from a variety of historical periods—and spaces. It is not just architects and traffic engineers who do this. The teams working with the model also include psychologists, social workers, artists and other professionals.

The model is available for viewing by visitors in Havana.

Recommended viewing—

La Maqueta de la Habana—http://youtu.be/6GAWLrY74Fk

La Maqueta de la Habana—http://youtu.be/ly_mRIK3ySO

Tourism

As a major source of income for Cuba, tourism brings visitors from all over the world. Almost. One nearby country with more than 300 million people forbids most of its residents (whether citizen or non-citizen) from traveling to Cuba.

Those who do visit Cuba, however, enjoy it immensely. They love the beaches, the ocean waters, the weather, the people, the food, the music, the drinks, the art, the architecture, and the countryside.

Cuba welcomes more than two million tourists a year

The most frequent visitors to Cuba are Canadians (945,000 in 2010), followed by those from the UK (174,000), then from other countries of Europe, South America and other areas of the world. [231] Comparatively few visitors are Americans, and even fewer are legal Americans, although with relaxed rules by the US government, Cuban-Americans have again become frequent visitors to Cuba.

Permanent residents of the US—citizens or not—cannot legally visit Cuba

The official regulations of the Office of Foreign Assets Control (OFAC) of the US Department of the Treasury state that the US government's sanctions against Cuba apply to: [232]

> All US citizens and permanent residents wherever they are located, all people and organizations physically in the United States, and all branches and subsidiaries of US organizations throughout the world.

Why does the US government prohibit Americans, and all permanent residents, from visiting Cuba?

> The Cuban Assets Control Regulations are issued under the Trading with the Enemy Act in response to certain hostile actions by the Cuban government [233]…The basic goal of the

---

[231] www.havanatimes.org/?p=60806

[232] Cuban Assets Control Regulations, 31 C.F.R. Part 515, (Revised September 30, 2004) are administered and enforced by the *Office of Foreign Assets Control* (OFAC).

[233] These "hostile actions" are unnamed.

sanctions is to isolate the Cuban government economically and deprive it of US dollars.

What are the penalties for violating these regulations?

Criminal penalties for violating the sanctions range up to 10 years in prison, $1,000,000 in corporate fines, and $250,000 in individual fines. Civil penalties up to $55,000 per violation may also be imposed.

Cuba is the only Communist country in the world that Americans are not allowed by their government to visit

The US Government does not restrict American citizens from visits to China, Laos, Vietnam or North Korea.

American tourists, corporations and dollars are allowed to visit, do business and live in China, a communist country of more than 1.3 billion people, yet American tourists, corporations and dollars are forbidden to set foot in Cuba, a communist country of less than 12 million people.

During the Cold War, when the United States considered the Soviet Union to be its greatest threat, the reason given for not allowing Americans to visit Cuba was that Cuba was an ally of the Soviet Union. Yet even at the height of the Cold War, the US government never placed any restrictions on Americans visiting the Soviet Union itself, the so-called "evil empire"—as declared by President Ronald Reagan. And they could also visit all other Communist countries in Eastern Europe.

Just not Cuba.

All other countries in the world allow their citizens to visit Cuba

The United States is the only developed country, and apparently the *only country at all,* that forbids its citizens to visit Cuba.

On the other hand, the government of Cuba welcomes you and anyone else who wishes to visit.

Cuban citizens are now freer to travel to the United States than US citizens are to Cuba

After years of restrictions on travel outside Cuba, Cubans can now travel wherever they wish, as far as the Cuban government is concerned. In January 2013, it lifted its restrictions on travel. Prior to this time, Cubans needed an expensive exit permit from the Cuban government and an invitation from their intended destination. Now they need only a valid passport and a visa from their destination country. Those Cubans who were previously allowed to travel could stay abroad only 11 months. Now 24 months is allowed. They can even live in other countries without losing their Cuban residency, provided they visit Cuba every two years.

Until now, the US has told Cuba "let your people go." The Cuban government now has. The dilemma for the US government is will they give a visa to any Cuban who wishes to visit the United States? And, since the US has its "wet foot-dry foot" policy allowing any Cuban who arrives on US land to remain in the country and eventually apply for residency, how will it deal with a possible large influx of Cubans? And how will it explain to its own people why Cubans have greater travel freedom than Americans, and why Cubans can visit the United States on their own, but those few Americans the US allows to visit Cuba must usually do so as part of a group tour.

If you are a Cuban-American, you can travel to Cuba whenever you wish. If you do not have Cuban relatives, you cannot

This "birth penalty" is a result of US foreign policy (actually *domestic* policy, since it penalizes only non-Cuban-Americans and others living in the United States.) Cuban-Americans can visit "close relatives" in Cuba whenever they wish. [234]

The US government claims that it does not really restrict travel to Cuba; it simply does not allow one to *spend money* in Cuba. It considers that anyone who stays in Cuba more than a day has spent money there. It is also illegal to receive goods or services for free from any Cuban national, so you cannot use an all-expense paid invitation as a way to circumvent the law.

The only way for most Americans to legally travel to Cuba is with a special license from OFAC. In 2011, an estimated 400,000 Americans traveled to Cuba. [235] Most of them were Cuban-Americans.

The US government does grant general licenses to certain classes of people for particular purposes. These include:

- Professional journalists on assignment in Cuba

---

[234] A "close relative" is any individual related to a person by blood, marriage, or adoption who is no more than three generations removed from that person or from a common ancestor with that person. For example, your mother's first cousin is your close relative for purposes of the Regulations, because you are both no more than three generations removed from your great-grandparents, who are the ancestors you have in common. Similarly, your husband's great-grandson is your close relative, because he is no more than three generations removed from your husband. However, your daughter's father-in-law is not your close relative, because you have no common ancestor. See § 515.339.
http://www.treasury.gov/resource-center/sanctions/Programs/Documents/cuba.pdf

[235] NPR   http://n.pr/SI9TQy

- Full-time professionals conducting academic research or attending professional conferences
- Persons on official government business

Specific licenses may be granted to such as:

- People visiting immediate family in Cuba
- Full-time graduate students conducting academic research to be counted toward a graduate degree
- Undergraduate or graduate students participating in a study-abroad program of at least ten weeks in length
- Professors or teachers employed at a US institution travelling to Cuba to teach
- People engaging in religious activities
- Freelance journalists
- People engaging in humanitarian projects
- People engaging in non-profit cultural exhibitions

Even Americans who visit Cuba on legal people-to-people programs may not go to the beach

If you are an American (or resident of the United States), you cannot travel to Cuba for purposes of *tourism*. As former US President George W. Bush said, "US law forbids Americans to travel to Cuba for pleasure." [236] (2003) Evidently, you are allowed to visit Cuba only for *dis*pleasure.

You may only attend educational and cultural activities where you can interact with the Cuban people. Interacting with them on the beach is evidently not allowed. (Naturally, if you are a Cuban-American, you can go to a Cuban beach whenever you want, as long as you want, whether you interact with Cubans on the beach or simply ignore them.)

The US government's Office of Financial Assets Control states that it will refuse a license to an organization that "wishes to sponsor and organize trips to Cuba in which travelers engage in individually-selected and/or self-directed activities." Ironically, the anti-Communist (but allegedly pro-individual) US government will not allow Americans in Cuba to act as self-directed individuals. Instead the licensing organization must prepare and require a "full-time schedule of activities in which the travelers will participate."

---

[236] http://2001-2009.state.gov/p/wha/rls/rm/25154.htm

Some Americans travel to Cuba illegally

Yes, it is done. US citizens and residents often travel to Cuba via countries such as Canada, Mexico or the Bahamas. These countries, however, have US customs agents to greet you on your return from Cuba, and Americans are required to have a license even if they fly to Cuba from a third country. For this reason some unlicensed travelers often travel via countries that do *not* have US customs stations, including Guatemala, Venezuela, Panama, Cayman Islands, Dominican Republic, Costa Rica and Haiti.

Reports are that few Americans are actually fined for visiting Cuba without a license. But some are. For the latest information on this, you are advised to do a Web search because the situation continually changes. Naturally, the author and publisher of this book advise you to remain within the law.

Recommended reading—

Organizations sponsoring people-to-people travel to Cuba (from the Latin America Working Group)
http://www.lawg.org/storage/documents/people2people.pdf

Cuba: What you need to know about US sanctions against Cuba, produced by the Office of Foreign Assets Control (OFAC)
http://www.treasury.gov/resource-center/sanctions/Programs/Documents/cuba.pdf

Cuban Government Customs Website—http://www.aduana.co.cu/

Recommended viewing—

Commercials for Americans who aren't allowed to see them on their own TV sets

Authentic Cuba (tourism ad)—http://youtu.be/6d2xGozti6s
Cuba Tourism Commercial—http://youtu.be/aftK1kWWSPs

Other guides—
Top 10 Attractions in Havana—http://youtu.be/EoCE8mHNY4M

Travel Guide on Cuba
Part 1: http://youtu.be/hbBoecdBBx4
Part 2: http://youtu.be/b2vLwy9dooY
Part 3: http://youtu.be/-MiZ8oSl03E

Canadian high school students visit Cuba
http://www.cubaexplorer.com/details/video_LB_new.php

Cuba for the Misinformed

José Martí International Airport, Havana, Cuba.
CREDIT: WIKIMEDIA COMMONS

Scheduled flights from thirty-three countries go to Cuba

Argentina
Bahamas
Belgium
Bolivia
Brazil
Canada
Chile
Colombia
Costa Rica
Dominican Republic
Ecuador
El Salvador
France
Germany
Guatemala
Honduras
Ireland
Italy
Jamaica
Japan
Mexico
Netherlands
Nicaragua
Panama
Peru
Portugal
Russia
Spain
Switzerland
Ukraine
United Kingdom
United States (charter)
Venezuela

Cuba has given permission to major American airlines to fly to Cuba, but they are not yet allowed to by the US government

Cuba has given United Airlines, American Airlines, Delta, JetBlue and US Airways the right to fly between most major US cities and Cuba, but the airlines do not yet have permission from the US government to actually do it. Cities approved include Atlanta, Baltimore, Chicago, Dallas, Houston, New Orleans, San Juan, and Tampa. There are a number of regular charter flights between some US cities (Miami, Los Angeles, New York, and Fort

Lauderdale) and Cuba, but those are only for the journalists, religious persons, Cuban-Americans, cultural tours and others who are allowed by the US government to visit Cuba.

Ernest Hemingway

One of Cuba's most popular tourist sites is Ernest Hemingway's home

American writer Ernest Hemingway moved to Cuba in 1939 and lived there for twenty-one years. He first stayed at Hotel Ambos Mundos in Havana (Room 511– which is now a small museum and can be visited by tourists.) Soon after, he bought a 15-acre farm on the ocean 15 miles from Havana. He named the property *Finca Vigia* (Lookout Farm) and it is now a very popular location for visiting tourists.

Living room at Hemingway's Finca Vigia.
CREDIT: INZWEIZEITEN / WIKIMEDIA COMMONS

In 1940 Hemingway established his summer home in Ketchum, Idaho but returned to his Cuba residence every winter. At Finca Vigia he wrote his novel *For Whom the Bell Tolls*. During World War II, when fishing on his boat, *Pilar*, off the Cuban coast, he was also looking for German submarines. His deep-sea fishing experiences led to his book *The Old Man and the Sea*, which was instrumental in his receiving the Nobel Prize in Literature in 1954. Hemingway left Cuba during the 1959 revolution, but returned occasionally.

Cuba for the Misinformed

Hemingway aboard the Pilar.
CREDIT: ERNEST HEMINGWAY PHOTOGRAPH COLLECTION,
JOHN F. KENNEDY PRESIDENTIAL LIBRARY

Recommended viewing—

Hemingway House—http://youtu.be/RdEOuqSE2WU

Michael Palin's Hemingway Adventure in Cuba
http://youtu.be/oW_1eE88MrU

Ernest Hemingway gave Fidel Castro a trophy

Ernest Hemingway met Fidel Castro briefly in 1960 when he awarded Castro a trophy in the Ernest Hemingway International Billfishing Tournament.

Hemingway and Castro
CREDIT: ARCHIVAL

Recommended viewing—

Fidel Castro and Ernest Hemingway after finishing contest (no audio)
http://youtu.be/nB-ffn8qHmg

There is a statue of Hemingway in a Havana bar

Reportedly, Hemingway's two favorite hangouts in Havana were both in *Habana Vieja* (Old Havana). One was *El Floridita*, on Obispo Street, the other *La Bodeguita del Medio*, on Empedrado Street. Each has a drink associated with Hemingway, as he allegedly once wrote, "My mojito in La Bodeguita. My daiquiri in El Floridita."

Although Hemingway may have written this statement, there is some doubt that he was a frequent visitor to *La Bodeguita*—if a visitor at all.

Cuba for the Misinformed

There is no doubt, however, that he was a frequent patron at *El Floridita*, as were other notables such as poet Ezra Pound, and writers John Dos Passos and Graham Greene. Today, when you visit the bar, you'll see a roped-off section at the left, next to the wall. Seated on a bar stool is a statue of Hemingway, permanently enjoying his Daiquiri, thanks to Cuban sculptor José Ramón Villa Soberón.

Statue of Hemingway by José Villa Soberón
at his usual bar stool at El Floridita, Havana.
CREDIT: FREDERIC SCHMALZBAUER /
WIKIMEDIA COMMONS

Hemingway (at end of bar in white shirt) at El Floridita with guests
including Spencer Tracy (on Hemingway's right).
CREDIT: ERNEST HEMINGWAY PHOTOGRAPH COLLECTION,
JOHN F. KENNEDY PRESIDENTIAL LIBRARY

Recommended viewing—

Michael Palin's Hemingway Adventure in Havana
http://youtu.be/IoUMeM5LI_o

El Floridita Bar—http://youtu.be/YRUvZIlSyEU

Varadero

Canadian and British tourists fly directly to the international airport at Cuba's biggest resort. Few Americans even know the resort exists

Varadero is Cuba's most popular tourist resort area, with as many as one million visitors a year enjoying more than twenty kilometers of white, sandy beaches. It is located on a peninsula 140 kilometers east of Havana. Varadero has more than a third of the hotel facilities on the entire island. It is also known as *Playa Azul* (Blue Beach), and is a popular diving and fishing area.

Entrance to Varadero beach
CREDIT: © KMIRAGAYA | DREAMSTIME.COM

Recommended viewing—

Varadero—http://youtu.be/zB13iqsTJus

Varadero—http://youtu.be/Ca23U7h_J58

Varadero Beach, Cuba.
CREDIT: WILDER MENDEZ / WIKIMEDIA COMMONS

Santiago de Cuba

In Santiago de Cuba one war ended. Fifty-five years later another began

Spanish troops were defeated here in 1898, ending the war called by the Americans the Spanish-American War. (The Cubans refer to it as the Spanish-Cuban-American War.) Fifty-five years later, another war began in Santiago de Cuba, when Fidel Castro launched his unsuccessful attack on the Moncada Barracks. A short time later, local teacher Frank País organized an anti-Batista movement which two years later merged with Fidel Castro's July 26 Movement and País took command of that movement in Oriente Province. In 1957 País was killed by Batista's police. He remains a great Cuban hero and the day of his and his brother's death (July 30) is celebrated as the *Day of the Martyrs of the Revolution*. On January 1, 1959, Fidel Castro proclaimed the victory of the Cuban Revolution from a balcony on Santiago's city hall.

Santiago is Cuba's second largest city, its second largest port (Havana is the largest), and the capital of Santiago de Cuba Province. Except for the entrance to Santiago de Cuba Bay, the municipality is surrounded by the mountains of the *Sierra Maestra*. It is these mountains that Fidel Castro and his forces used as their base for their efforts to overthrow Fulgencio Batista.

243

Santiago at night
CREDIT: ALEX CANO/WIKIMEDIA COMMONS

French plantation owners took refuge here after the Haitian Slave Revolt of 1791. The mix of French, Spanish and African has created a unique and lively city known for its music, its dance, and the annual *Carnaval*, held in July. Cuba's writer-hero José Martí is buried here at the Cementerio Santa Efigenia.

Cathedral of Santiago de Cuba
CREDIT: CVBR/WIKIMEDIA COMMONS

World Heritage Sites

Cuba has nine World Heritage Sites

A World Heritage Site is defined by UNESCO as a location having special cultural or natural significance. These sites are to be protected—particularly in times of war—because of their value to the international community. The Cuban sites are: [237]

Old Havana (*La Habana Vieja*) and its Fortifications

Province of Ciudad de la Habana

Havana was founded in 1519 by the Spanish. By the 17th century, it had become one of the Caribbean's main centres for ship-building. Although it is today a sprawling metropolis of 2 million inhabitants, its old centre retains an interesting mix of Baroque and neoclassical monuments, and a homogeneous ensemble of private houses with arcades, balconies, wrought-iron gates and internal courtyards.

Website—http://whc.unesco.org/en/list/204

Trinidad and the Valley de los Ingenios

Province of Sancti Spiritus

Founded in the early 16th century in honour of the Holy Trinity, the city was a bridgehead for the conquest of the American continent. Its 18th- and 19th-century buildings, such as the Palacio Brunet and the Palacio Cantero, were built in its days of prosperity from the sugar trade.

Website—http://whc.unesco.org/en/list/460

San Pedro de la Roca Castle in Santiago de Cuba

Province of Santiago de Cuba

Commercial and political rivalries in the Caribbean region in the 17th century resulted in the construction of this massive series of fortifications on a rocky promontory, built to protect the important port of Santiago. This intricate complex of forts, magazines, bastions and batteries is the most

---

[237] http://whc.unesco.org/en/statesparties/cu

complete, best-preserved example of Spanish-American military architecture, based on Italian and Renaissance design principles.

Website—http://whc.unesco.org/en/list/841

Descembarco del Granma National Park (where the revolutionaries' boat *Granma* landed)

South-east corner of the Republic of Cuba

Desembarco del Granma National Park, with its uplifted marine terraces and associated ongoing development of karst topography and features, represents a globally significant example of geomorphologic and physiographic features and ongoing geological processes. The area, which is situated in and around Cabo Cruz in south-east Cuba, includes spectacular terraces and cliffs, as well as some of the most pristine and impressive coastal cliffs bordering the western Atlantic.

Website—http://whc.unesco.org/en/list/889

Viñales Valley

Province of Pinar del Rio

The Viñales valley is encircled by mountains and its landscape is interspersed with dramatic rocky outcrops. Traditional techniques are still in use for agricultural production, particularly of tobacco. The quality of this cultural landscape is enhanced by the vernacular architecture of its farms and villages, where a rich multi-ethnic society survives, illustrating the cultural development of the islands of the Caribbean, and of Cuba.

Website—http://whc.unesco.org/en/list/840

The Archaeological Landscape of the First Coffee Plantations in the Southeast of Cuba

Santiago and Guantanamo Provinces

The remains of the 19th-century coffee plantations in the foothills of the Sierra Maestra are unique evidence of a pioneer form of agriculture in a difficult terrain. They throw considerable light on the economic, social, and technological history of the Caribbean and Latin American region.

Website—http://whc.unesco.org/en/list/1008

Alejandro de Humboldt National Park

Guantánamo and Holguín Provinces

Complex geology and varied topography have given rise to a diversity of ecosystems and species unmatched in the insular Caribbean and created one of the most biologically diverse tropical island sites on earth. Many of the underlying rocks are toxic to plants so species have had to adapt to survive in these hostile conditions. This unique process of evolution has resulted in the development of many new species and the park is one of the most important sites in the Western Hemisphere for the conservation of endemic flora. Endemism of vertebrates and invertebrates is also very high.

Website—http://whc.unesco.org/en/list/839

Urban Historic Centre of Cienfuegos

Municipality of Cienfuegos

The colonial town of Cienfuegos was founded in 1819 in the Spanish territory but was initially settled by immigrants of French origin. It became a trading place for sugar cane, tobacco and coffee. Situated on the Caribbean coast of southern-central Cuba at the heart of the country's sugar cane, mango, tobacco and coffee production area, the town first developed in the neoclassical style. It later became more eclectic but retained a harmonious overall townscape. Among buildings of particular interest are the Government Palace (City Hall), San Lorenzo School, the Bishopric, the Ferrer Palace, the former lyceum, and some residential houses. Cienfuegos is the first, and an outstanding example of an architectural ensemble representing the new ideas of modernity, hygiene and order in urban planning as developed in Latin America from the 19th century.

Website—http://whc.unesco.org/en/list/1202

Historic Centre of Camagüey

Camagüey Province

One of the first seven villages founded by the Spaniards in Cuba, Camagüey played a prominent role as the urban centre of an inland territory dedicated to cattle breeding and the sugar industry. Settled in its current location in 1528, the town developed on the basis of an irregular urban pattern that contains a system of large and minor squares, serpentine streets, alleys and irregular urban blocks, highly exceptional for Latin American colonial towns located in plain territories. The 54 ha Historic Centre of Camagüey constitutes an exceptional example of a traditional urban settlement relatively isolated from main trade routes. The Spanish colonizers followed medieval European influences in terms of urban layout and traditional construction techniques brought to the Americas by their masons and construction masters. The property reflects the influence of numerous styles through the ages: neoclassical, eclectic, Art Deco, Neo-colonial as well as some Art Nouveau and rationalism.

Website—http://whc.unesco.org/en/list/1270

Zunzún

Cuba is home to the world's smallest bird, the "bee hummingbird"

Cubans call it the *zunzún* ("buzzbuzz") or even *zunzuncito* ("little buzzbuzz"). The zunzún is about two inches long and weighs less than a penny—about 5/100ths of an ounce (1.8 grams). Because of its small size, visitors often at first think it is a bee.

Recommended viewing—

Zunzún y Zunzuncito—http://youtu.be/-348UxJsW7Q

What Next?

For more than half a century, the Cuban government has used the US government as an excuse for Cuba's shortcomings, for its lack of food, for its lack of medical supplies, for its lack of resources to rebuild housing, for its repression of communication with the outside and of free speech, for its refusal to formally recognize opposition parties, and numerous other problems in Cuban society. Cubans say, "The problem is the US embargo...The problem is US aggression...The problem is that for more than fifty years the United States has been trying to overthrow the government of Cuba."

The excuse is valid.

The US government *has* done its best to destroy Cuba. It claims that its target is the Cuban government, not the Cuban people, yet it is the people who have been the direct victims of US policies. The US government says that the Cuban people should have the freedom of choice, yet it does not accept the choices the Cuban people have already made.

This is not to say that the US government is solely responsible for the problems of Cuba. Hardly. Many of the problems in Cuba have been self-inflicted. The Castro government solidified its hold on the government after the successful revolution by executing not just members of the Batista government, military and police who were guilty of crimes, but of executing, imprisoning or driving into exile those who fought on the side of the revolution but who did not wish to see a Communist government replace Batista.

The revolutionary government closed down all small businesses, thereby destroying the middle class, which has been a key to stability and democracy in many other countries. It adopted the Soviet model of central government planning, which had already proved elsewhere to have serious failings. And, while it created a form of citizen involvement at a level not seen in many Western democracies, it set parameters on this involvement which sharply

Cuba for the Misinformed

restricted the range of ideas and options which could be discussed: "Inside the Revolution, everything; outside, nothing." [238]

The Americans have indeed established harsh measures toward Cuba—the Bay of Pigs invasion, the bombing of hotels and other businesses, the destruction of sugar cane fields and other crops, the plans and attempts to assassinate Cuba's president—all actions that are criminal under international law. It unilaterally canceled its sugar purchase contracts with Cuba—driving Cuba into the economic arms of the Soviet Union—then prohibited American citizens from visiting Cuba, thus eliminating Cuba's income from those tourists.

Responding to the actions of the American government, the Cuban government in turn developed harsh measures internally. If the United States chose to be at war with Cuba, then Cuba had no choice but to act as if it were at war (an essentially *defensive* one) with the United States. As the Americans, primarily through use of Cuban exiles in Florida, launched a variety of ongoing attacks on people, crops, businesses and industries in Cuba, the Cuban government was often forced to adopt harsh measures to protect its people and itself—to the point of treating a number of its citizens as if they were in league with the enemy (and a number of them often were.)

The US treatment of Cuba has been a convenient, and often extremely justified, excuse for Cuba's problems and its often rigid internal policies. Cuba, however, has also been a convenient excuse for the Americans.

For more than a century, the word "communist" has struck fear in American hearts. Having a communist government just ninety miles offshore is a mixed blessing for the US government. While American business sees Cuba as a desirable market—11 million potential customers—the American government sees Cuba as a living and very convenient example of the dangers of communism. Cuba has been enshrined by the US government as the last living relic of the Cold War. It is a reminder that as bad as conditions in the United States might get, it is still better than Cuba: a presumed result of the virtues of capitalism and American-style democracy versus the vices of socialism and communism.

The logical conclusion from fifty years of American actions towards Cuba is that US governments have *not* wanted change in Cuba. Putting a country or a government on the defensive is quite obviously not how to bring about change. No one, particularly a country, responds well to such pressure. It simply makes people—and countries—more intransigent. Had the US government really wanted change in Cuba, it would have shut down the embargo, permitted US businesses to operate in Cuba, and allowed all Americans to visit Cuba—just as people from other countries in the world have always been able to do.

---

[238] www.worldaffairsjournal.org/article/cuban-days-inscrutable-nation

Doing so would have placed all of the responsibility on Cuba. Cuba would have had to deal with the demands of international and US businesses for unrestricted trade and investment; with the demands of American tourists for American-style restaurants, hotels, and other attractions; and with the demands of Cubans for an American style of life and all of the consumer and entertainment goods entailed. It could have been a disaster for Cuban culture, and most likely would have been for Cuba's political and economic system.

What does this mean? Does it mean that neither the Cuban government nor the US government sincerely wants a change in policy? Does it imply a symbiotic relationship in which a continuing embargo is essential for both?

Perhaps we will never know. What we do know is that for decades the US government has proclaimed that Cuba uses the embargo as an excuse for its failings.

We can never know what might have happened if the US government had supported Cuba after its revolution. Or at least been neutral. It was the time of the Cold War, when most countries were forced to choose to be allied either with the US or with the USSR. The US aggressively rejected Cuba, and Cuba was thus forced to turn to the USSR for assistance. A different attitude on the part of the US could have led to a very different Cuban history—and a very different relationship with the United States.

But that was then. We cannot know a different past, but we can find out in the future what might happen in Cuba if the US government were to change its stance now. If the US government changes its policies toward Cuba, it will present Cuba with many more options; options that have not been available for more than fifty years. Should Cuba, after another decade, not take advantage of these options, the US could rightfully say, "See, we told you so." But without the US changing its position now, that will never be possible, and we will never know.

If the US government truly believes its claim that Cuba uses the embargo as an all-purpose excuse, all the US needs to do is *end the embargo*—immediately—and announce to the world that Cuba's excuse no longer exists. The American president simply needs to say, "We have ended the embargo. The Cuban government's excuse is gone. An excuse which we have always believed is phony. Let us now see how the Cuban government treats its people *without* that excuse. We and the world await the results."

Resources

Suggestions for other sources of information on Cuba, some of which are mentioned in this book.

Books

Brenner, Phillip, Jimenez Marguerite Rose, John M. Kir, and William M. Leo Grande (eds.), *A Contemporary Cuba Reader: Reinventing the Revolution,* (Lanham MD: Rowman and Littlefield 2007)

Castro, Fidel and Ramonet, Ignacio, *Fidel Castro: My Life* (New York: Scribner 2008)

Franklin, Jane, *Cuba and the United States: A Chronological History (Melbourne: Ocean Press 1997)* Available as PDF at http://janefranklin.info/Cuba.htm

García Luis, Leo, *Cuban Revolution Reader: A Documentary History of 40 Key Moments of the Cuban Revolution,* (Melbourne: Ocean Press 2001)

Keeble, Alexandra (Ed.), *In the Spirit of Wandering Teachers,* Cuban Literacy Campaign 1961, (Melbourne: Ocean Press 2001)

Lizra, Chen, *My Seductive Cuba* (Vancouver: Latidos Productions 2011)

Loviny, Christopher and Alessandra Silvestri-Levy, *Cuba: by Korda,* (Melbourne: Ocean Press 2006)

Martinez Puentes, Silva, *Cuba: Beyond our Dreams,* (Havana: Editorial José Martí 2004)

Saney, Isaac, *Cuba: A Revolution in Motion,* (Black Point NS, Canada: Fernwood 2004)

Schoultz, Lars, That Infernal Little Cuban Republic: The United States and the Cuban Revolution (Chapel Hill: University of North Carolina Press 2009)

Stout, Nancy, *One Day in December,* (New York: Monthly Review Press 2013)

Film

"Fidel" and other films
A 1969 documentary on Fidel Castro
www.saullandau.com

"Fidel"
A 2001 documentary on Fidel Castro
www.estelabravo.com

"Maestra"
A documentary on the Cuban Literacy Campaign
www.maestrathefilm.org/

"Simply Korda"
A documentary on Cuban photographer Alberto Korda
www.havana-cultura.com/en/nl/visual-art/photographer/alberto-korda

Cuba for the Misinformed

"The Power of Community: How Cuba survived Peak Oil"
A documentary on the "Special Period"
www.powerofcommunity.org

638 Ways to Kill Castro
British TV documentary (2006)
http://freedocumentaries.org/int.php?filmID=353

Websites

AfroCubaWeb
Comprehensive website on AfroCuban music and culture
www.afrocubaweb.com

Along the Malecón
Blog by American journalist/academic. Also hosts Cuba Money Project (see below).
www.alongthemalecon.blogspot.com/

Authentic Cuba Travel
Canada-based website specializing in educational, cultural and nature tours
www.authenticubatours.com

Avistamientos
Online gallery of contemporary Cuban art
www.cubartecontemporaneo.com

Canadian Network on Cuba
Network formed to bring together Canadians who share an affection for Cuba and Cubans.
www.canadiannetworkoncuba.ca

Capitol Hill Cubans
"An insider's view on US policy" - strongly anti-Castro
www.capitolhillcubans.com/

Center for Cuban Studies
"Dedicated to providing information about contemporary Cuba and contributing to a normalization of relations between Cuba and the United States."
www.cubaupdate.org

Che Guevara Internet Archive
Library, biography, images, speeches
www.marxists.org/archive/guevara/index.htm

Compañero Che
Webite devoted to Che Guevara
www.companeroche.com

Council for Foreign Relations
"Independent, non-partisan" think tank – Publishes *Foreign Affairs* bi-monthly journal
www.cfr.org/region/cuba/ri213

Cuba
BBC Country Profile
http://news.bbc.co.uk/2/hi/americas/country_profiles/1203299.stm

Cuba
US Central Intelligence Agency World Factbook
www.cia.gov/library/publications/the-world-factbook/geos/cu.html

Cuba
Travel information from Lonely Planet
www.lonelyplanet.com/cuba

Cuba
US State Department Country Specific Information
http://travel.state.gov/travel/cis_pa_tw/cis/cis_1097.html

Cuba
Comprehensive Wikipedia website
http://en.wikipedia.org/wiki/Cuba

Cuba Absolutely
Web magazine with articles, stories and photos on art, culture, music, dance, travel, business and more in Havana and throughout Cuba.
www.cubaabsolutely.com

Cubarte
"The portal of Cuban culture"
www.cubarte-english.cult.cu

Cuba Bug, The
Blog of British academic and frequent traveler to Cuba
http://thecubabug.blogspot.com

Cuba Central
Organization that is "Devoted to changing US policy toward the countries of the Americas by basing our relations on mutual respect"
http://cubacentral.wordpress.com/

Cuba Education Tours
Cuba education and culture tours. Based in Canada but also sends Americans to Cuba on legal people-to-people cultural encounters.
www.cubaeducationtours.com

Cuba Journal
"News, opinion and more about Cuba"
http://cubajournal.blogspot.com

Cuba Junky
"Goal is to help travelers to get the most out of their visit/vacation to Cuba"
www.cuba-junky.com

Cubalinda
Flights, hotels, tours,
www.cubalinda.com/

Cuba Mapa.com
Maps of Cuba
www.cubamapa.com/

Cuba Money Project
Investigative journalism on US government-financed programs to change Cuba's government
http://cubamoneyproject.org/

CubaNews
A wide range of news and information about the island, the Cuban community abroad, Cuba's international relations, and related topics
http://groups.yahoo.com/group/CubaNews/

Cuba for the Misinformed

Cuba News
Cuba-related news with a primary focus on business information
www.cubanews.com

Cubanow
Cuban and culture news
www.cubanow.net

Cuba Sanctions
US Department of Treasury
www.treasury.gov/resource-center/sanctions/programs/pages/cuba.aspx

Cuba Si
Extensive official news from Cuba
http://news.cubasi.cu

Cuba Solidarity Campaign
Campaigns in the UK against the US blockade of Cuba and for the Cuban peoples' right to
self-determination and sovereignty
http://www.cuba-solidarity.org.uk/

Cuba Tourist Board in Canada
Comprehensive information for the prospective visitor. Includes videos.
www.gocuba.ca

Cuban 5
International Committee for the Freedom of the Cuban 5
www.thecuban5.org

Cuban Art News
Private foundation that promotes education, appreciation, and a deepening understanding of
Cuban art and culture
www.cubanartnews.org/

Cuban News Agency
Social, economic, political, sports and cultural news from Cuba
www.cubanews.ain.cu/

Cubaninsider
Website from a self-described "fiercely pro-democracy conservative Republican"
http://cubaninsider.blogspot.com/

Cuban Journalists Blogs (*Blogs Periodistas Cubanos*)
A directory of many Cuban blogs on policy, culture and society, journalism and technology,
photograph, history and tradition, sexuality, and general. (Spanish)
http://blogcip.cu/

Cuban Triangle
Havana-Miami-Washington events and arguments and their impact on Cuba
http://cubantriangle.blogspot.com/

Cuba versus Blockade
Website calling for end to blockade
www.cubavsbloqueo.cu/Default.aspx?tabid=1624

Cubaweb
Tourist directory of Cuba from Cuba's Ministry of Tourism
www.cubaweb.cu/en

DTCuba (Tourist Directory of Cuba)
Private tour operator offering tourist information and news
www.dtcuba.com/Default.aspx?lng=2

Floridita
Havana's famous restaurant and bar
www.floridita-cuba.com/

Fodor's
Fodor's online Cuba travel guide
www.fodors.com/world/caribbean/cuba/

Free the Five
National Committee to Free the Cuba Five
www.freethefive.org/

Frommer's
Frommer's online guide to Cuba
www.frommers.com/destinations/cuba/

Generation Y
Blog of Yoani Sánchez, highly-publicized Cuban dissident.
http://www.desdecuba.com/generationy/

Global Exchange
An international human rights organization dedicated to promoting social, economic and
environmental justice around the world. Leads trips to Cuba.
www.globalexchange.org

Granma
Official newspaper of the Central Committee of the Cuban Communist Party
www.granma.cu

Habanos
Cuban cigars
www.habanos.com

Havana Club Rum
Official website
www.havana-club.com

Havana Cultura
Havana artists presented by Havana Club Rum
www.havana-cultura.com

Havana Note
A group blog covering various corners of the cultural, political, military and economic
dimensions of US-Cuba relations. Goal is to take advantage of recent developments in Cuba
and the United States to redirect US-Cuba policy and relations toward a more sensible,
mutually beneficial direction.
www.thehavananote.com

Havana Reporter
Online weekly newspaper from the Prensa Latina News Agency
http://www.plenglish.com/images/stories/Media/TheHavanaReporter.pdf

Havana Times
A wide-ranging publication open to various opinions about Cuban reality and to the frank
discussion of proposals for the present and the future of the nation and the world. An
outstanding news and opinion site.
www.havanatimes.org

Cuba for the Misinformed

Here is Havana
Blog of an American journalist living in Cuba.
http://hereishavana.wordpress.com/

Buy the iPhone app – Havana Good Time
http://itunes.apple.com/app/havana-good-time/id385663683?mt=8

History of Cuba
500 years of Cuban history
www.historyofcuba.com

Insight Cuba
"Legal people-to-people travel for Americans between the US and Cuba"
www.insightcuba.com

International Institute for the Study of Cuba
Initiative by a team of UK-located academics, specialists and consultants with the object of providing an in-depth and focused appraisal of the Cuban "Social Experience."
www.cubastudies.org

Jane Franklin
Entire Cuban history book downloadable for free as PDF
www.janefranklin.info

Killing Hope
Website on US foreign policy by author William Blum
www.killinghope.org

Latin American Studies – Cuba
Huge list of links to a wide variety of information
http://latinamericanstudies.org/cuba.htm

Latin America Working Group
Non-profit advocacy organization working to "change US policies towards Latin America and promote human rights, justice, peace and sustainable development throughout the region."
www.lawg.org

Lexington Institute
"A nonprofit, nonpartisan public policy research organization"
http://www.lexingtoninstitute.org/cuba

Lonely Planet
Lonely Planet's online guide to Cuba
www.lonelyplanet.com/cuba

Moon Travel Guide
Moon's online guide to Cuba
www.moon.com/destinations/cuba/discover-cuba

National Committee to Free the Cuban Five
Working to "create public awareness of the anti-terrorist mission of the Cuban Five, and to create support for the demand that the United States government should free the Cuban Five and let them return to Cuba."
www.freethefive.org/

National Security Archive
"Public interest law firm defending and expanding public access to government information, global advocate of open government, and indexer and publisher of former secrets."
http://www.gwu.edu/~nsarchiv/

Nation Master – Cuba
A vast collection of statistics
www.nationmaster.com/country/cu-cuba

Ocean Press
"Radical books on Latin America and the world"
www.oceanbooks.com.au/

Pastors for Peace
Delivers humanitarian aid to Latin America and the Caribbean. Contact in the United States
for Cuba's Latin American School of Medicine.
www.ifconews.org/

Prensa Latina News Agency
Latin American news agency with headquarters in Havana and 28 bureaus worldwide
www.plenglish.com/

Progreso Weekly
Online magazine with news and columnists
www.progreso-weekly.com

Project Censored
The issues ignored by mainstream US media
www.projectcensored.org

Radio Free Cuba
Cuban music by Cuban artists, 24 hours a day
(hosted by the author of this book)
www.radiofreecuba.com

Radio Habana Cuba
Spanish broadcasts. Articles in English, Spanish, French, Portuguese, Esperanto and Arabic.
www.rhc.cu/ing/

Rough Guides
Rough Guide online guide to Cuba
www.roughguides.com/travel/central-america-and-the-caribbean/cuba.aspx/

Translating Cuba
English translations of Cuban bloggers
www.translatingcuba.com

United States Interests Section – Havana, Cuba
US government representatives in Cuba
http://havana.usint.gov/

US Women & Cuba Collaboration
"Association of women and organizations working in coalition with women in Cuba to build
bridges within and between our nations that foster inclusive and progressive women's
movements and networks for justice, real security and women's rights."
www.womenandcuba.org/

Walter Lippmann
Personal website from a writer/photographer with extensive information and news on Cuba.
Lippmann maintains the daily report from the CubaNews Yahoo group (see above).
www.walterlippmann.com/

What you need to know about US Sanctions against Cuba
Overview of the Cuban Assets Control Regulations
www.treasury.gov/resource-center/sanctions/Programs/Documents/cuba.pdf

Radio Free Cuba

Music. Not propaganda.

Radio Free Cuba was the original name for a US government radio station intended to beam propaganda into Cuba. That station became known as Radio Marti, which still exists, although it is jammed by the Cuban government and few Cubans hear, or are interested in hearing, the station.

Radio Free Cuba is now a private station on the Web run by the author of this book. At www.RadioFreeCuba.com you can hear Cuban music by Cuban artists 24 hours a day.

At this website you will also find an extensive collection of links to Cuba-relevant websites.

www.radiofreecuba.com

Index

Index

Cuba for the Misinformed

Photo Credits

Adam Jones Adamjones.Freeservers.Com
Alberto Korda
Alejandro Cuba Ruiz /Wikimedia Commons
Aleksandar Todorovic/Bigstock
Alex Cano/Wikimedia Commons
Antonio Milena—ABR/Wikimedia Commons
Art Market Monitor
Barry Evans https://picasaweb.google.com/117271110082174811511
Beat Muttenzer/Flickr
Bill Weaver/Narcosphere
Bluesypete/Wikimedia Commons
Caridad/Havana Times
Carlos Reusser Monsalvez/Flickr
Central Bank Of Cuba
Central Intelligence Agency
Cuban Institute of Cinematographic Art and Industry
College Library
Cubanfoodmarket.com
CVBR/Wikimedia Commons
Dan Deluca/Flickr
David Shankbone / Wikimedia Commons
Detznaga/Wikimedia Commons
Dirk Van Der Made/Wikimedia Commons
Duncan Cameron/National Archives of Canada
Dzain/Bigstock
Ernest Hemingway Photograph Collection, John F. Kennedy Presidential Library
Ernesto Guevara Lynch/Wikimedia Commons
Fernando Trueba Producciones, Estudio Mariscal And Magic Light Pictures
Freddy Alborta
Frederic Schmalzbauer / Wikimedia Commons
Global Exchange
H.L. Matthews Papers, Rare Book and Manuscript Library, Columbia
Ian Usher/Flickr http://flic.kr/p/6hHnYy
Inzweizeiten / Wikimedia Commons
Jean-Pierre Dalbéra/Wikipedia
Jim/Wikimedia Commons
Jorge Royan http://www.royan.com.ar
Jose Gomez-Sicre Photographic Archives
Kamira/Bigstock
Kmiragaya | Dreamstime.Com
Krokodyl / Wikimedia Commons
Latin American Medical School
Luis Korda
Lukas Mathis/Wikimedia Commons
Mark Scott Johnson/Wikimedia Commons
Marshall Soules www.marshallsoules.ca

Wikimedia Commons images

I came to Casablanca for the waters.

The waters? What waters? We're in the desert.

I was misinformed.

"Casablanca" (1942)

You may purchase copies of the paperback version of Cuba for the Misinformed at:

- www.cubamisinformed.com
- Amazon.com
- Barnes & Noble.com
- all booksellers

Digital versions (Kindle, epub) are also available at:

www.cubamisinformed.com

CPSIA information can be obtained at www.ICGtesting.com
Printed in the USA
LVOW12s2100061213

364227LV00007B/191/P